THE GLASGOW STORY

"THE CAUR"

THE GLASGOW STORY

by

COLM BROGAN

PICTORIAL AIDS BY
KEIR

FREDERICK MULLER LTD.
LONDON

FIRST PUBLISHED BY FREDERICK MULLER LTD.
IN 1952
PRINTED IN GREAT BRITAIN BY EBENEZER BAYLIS AND SON, LTD.
THE TRINITY PRESS, WORCESTER AND LONDON
BOUND BY THE DORSTEL PRESS LTD. HARLOW

CONTENTS

Details of Illustrations
Frontispiece

CHAPTER | PAGE
1. THE FAME OF THE CITY 7
2. THE PLACE 16
3. THE PEOPLE 27
4. THE GLASGOW MAN 38
5. THE GLASGOW WOMAN 55
6. WORK 65
7. PRAYER 87
8. EDUCATION 105
9. THE UNIVERSITY 122
10. CULTURE 146
11. FUN AND GAMES 158
12. THE PROBLEM 179
13. POLITICS 197
14. THEY BELONG TO GLASGOW . . . 217

CHAPTER ONE

THE FAME OF THE CITY

THERE are few who would deny that Glasgow enjoys a rather special regard throughout a large part of the world. This is not the delusion of a native son, though it must be admitted that such delusions are common. Some of the inhabitants of Leeds are weak enough to imagine that the particular virtues and character of their city are a frequent subject of conversation in Melbourne and Shanghai. There are Manchester men who take it for granted that the Ship Canal, the *Guardian* and the Midland Hotel are three of the seven wonders of the modern world. I once spent the best part of an evening listening to a circumstantial account of the varied and vital impact made by men from Burton-on-Trent on the entire civilized world. I was staying in Burton-on-Trent at the time.

There is no harm in these fancies, but rather some good, if it reconciles people to their lot. Living in Leeds may be more cheerfully borne by those who are under the delusion that humanity thinks much of and about Leeds. But living in Leeds without that delusion must be a tedious, wearing and unprofitable effort, like standing on your head at a party while all the other guests have turned their backs on you to look at the television.

However, there is no fancy about the special interest so many people have in Glasgow. It is a fact. That is not to say it is a complimentary fact. The novel *No Mean City* was a story of razor-slashing and sordid sex conducted against a background of stair-head lavatories out of order. No doubt the ballet *Miracle of the Gorbals* has a more studied æsthetic approach, but I understand that the theme is much the same. The most popular of all books on Glasgow was called *Cancer of Empire*. It created a lot of interest, but anyone who calls that interest flattering is easily pleased.

But it is a principle of modern life that any kind of publicity is better than no publicity, and Glasgow certainly gets plenty, and not all of it unfavourable. I am told that during the Prohibition period American cinema audiences were apt to laugh and cheer at any mention or glimpse of Glasgow on the screen. They knew Glasgow as a city which produced whisky they could drink with confidence that their stomach lining would remain more or less where it was before. It was a gratifying and well-deserved testimonial.

Of course, a sensitive Glasgow man might suspect an unsatisfactory undertone in the warm American laughter. If the Americans had full confidence in the quality of Glasgow whisky, that implied a pleasing faith in Glasgow honesty, but perhaps it also implied something else. When a guest passes out completely at a party, there is always some other guest who is unanimously entrusted with the delicate and difficult task of restoring him to some superficial resemblance to human life. He is acknowledged to be an expert in saving and mysterious arts, but there are some kinds of knowledge which are not acquired in dull classrooms. They are acquired in what is poetically known as the University of Life, where field-work comprises the entire curriculum. The man with a good degree in this

form of resuscitation is known to have learned his lessons
the hard way, and Glasgow may have the reputation of
being a reliable whisky-producer because it also has the
reputation of being an enthusiastic whisky-consumer. So,
at least, a sensitive Glasgow man might suspect. Fortunately, sensitive Glasgow men are in strikingly short supply.

Undoubtedly, Glasgow has a reputation for exceedingly
heavy drinking. This reputation is partly the result of the
confession of Scottish comedians who are foo the noo,
with a wee deoch an' doris while Glasgow goes round and
round. It is partly the result of the behaviour of the International crowds who come to Wembley every second year.
It is partly the result of unbridled and highly imaginative
temperance propaganda. It is also partly the result of the
fact that Glasgow people drink a lot.

Violence is another part of the Glasgow story, and it
must be said that the Press of Britain has done a good deal
to confirm the popular belief. In the matter of violence,
the ordinary canons of journalism are suspended for
Glasgow, where "Dog bites man" is news. The most
ordinary assault on the police is apt to find its way into
some London newspaper if it happens in Glasgow. At
one Glasgow election meeting a pistol was fired. This
was considered worthy of headlines over Britain. True,
it was a toy pistol, but still, it was fired in Glasgow.

With the name for violence goes the name for revolutionary activity. There was a time when worthy matrons
in Bournemouth and Cheltenham shuddered at the lank
locks and the staring eye of James Maxton, and waited for
the day when "Red Clydeside" would justify its title in
flames and blood. More sagacious heads than are to be
found among the female *bourgeoisie* have been filled with

much the same notion. A prominent Glasgow man, returning across the Atlantic, made friends with an American business-man who was coming to Britain to prospect
for a factory site. The Glasgow man promptly went into
action with a glowing and truthful account of the advantages of a Glasgow site, but the American refused even to
listen. He knew about Glasgow. That was the place where
the Reds and the yeggs came from. That was the place he
meant to stay out of.

It has also been said with a semblance of plausibility
that the industrial prospects of Glasgow have sometimes
been damaged by the strong disinclination of certain
middle-class women to settle anywhere near it. These
women are the wives of executives and other big-shots in
the industrial and commercial world, and they use all
their feminine arts to persuade their husbands to settle
down and open up business in some more agreeable part
of the world.

They say Glasgow is terribly and exceptionally ugly.
(Manchester women have said so.) They say Glasgow is
terribly and exceptionally dirty. (Liverpool women have
uttered these words.) They say that life in Glasgow is
raucous, rude and rowdy, the local culture meagre and
low, the local accent uncouth and the local vocabulary fit
only for the ears of policemen and psycho-analysts. It is
not only the female English who say these things. It is
not only the English. I once knew a Highlander of some
distinction who used to make considerable detours in his
journeys to avoid the bitter need to change trains in
Glasgow. To this silent snub one can only retort that
there are some men in Glasgow who would make even
bigger detours to avoid meeting a Highlander.

Dirty, violent, alcoholic, Bolshie, dull, dreary, wet and windy. If this were all of Glasgow's reputation, there would be small cause for self-congratulation in the Second City. But it is not all. There are some people who say "Ah!" when they hear you come from Glasgow. They don't say "Really", or "How nice" or "How interesting". They just say "Ah!", but that "Ah!" is a mouthful. It expresses all those little points of trifling criticism hinted at above.

But there are other people who react quite differently. These are mainly men who have spent some time in Glasgow. Strangers in English pubs have recognized my accent and told me, almost with tears, of the merry days and nights they had spent in Glasgow. They sighed for a freer air, or more liberal spirit and a more pungent joviality than they could find in their native land. The accent didn't worry them at all, for it was more than an accent. They took it for a foreign language and they rubbed along very well without it. Little peculiarities of speech and behaviour that would have shattered them in a fellow-Englishman disturbed them not at all, but were accepted as part of local custom and recollected with chuckling appreciation of something rich and strange.

I once spoke to a young soldier who was born and bred in genuinely metropolitan London. He had begun his army career in Bournemouth and then had been transferred to Glasgow. When I suggested that he must have regretted the change, he looked at me as if I had suddenly been bereft of my senses, if any. Bournemouth he regarded as a kind of semi-final for the cemetery, but Glasgow was alive, pulsing with *bonhomie* and uninhibited enjoyment of this, that and the other. He had had the best time of his life in Glasgow, and the London that he knew was a flat and friendless place in comparison.

It must be admitted that his response was not universal. Evelyn Waugh, for example, has indicated in *Brideshead Revisited* that he did not enjoy his period of service on the outskirts of Glasgow. In one of his short stories Aldous Huxley has suggested, in effect, that Glasgow reminds him of the more depressing of *Grimm's Fairy Tales*.

These men are not alone, but they are few. The hosts of the Common Man are against them, and literally millions of the Common Man have voted it the best town in Britain for a fighting man to stay in. The inhabitants of many other towns have made the same claim, but it must be insisted that this is just another of those fancies that do no harm, so long as they are not carried too far. Whatever the fighting men said about other towns from mere politeness, what they said about Glasgow was what they really meant. That is a truth not to be argued about. You must take it or leave it. In fact, you must take it.

Yet, it may perhaps be conceded that the native sometimes finds the enthusiasm of Glasgow's friends nearly as puzzling as the strong aversion of Glasgow's enemies. It is not true to say that Glasgow is specially ugly. But, is it true to say that Glasgow is specially gay?

Eglinton Street on a wet Sunday evening. The shadow of the railway wall falls half-way across the gleaming tramlines. On one side there is nothing but the wall, except the church which the railway has neatly sliced in half. On the other side the blank tenements stand in rigid dreary line and their stone seems to suck in whatever light there may be. Except for an occasional dingy newsagent's or pub, the tenements are as blank as the opposite wall, and they go on and on. Overhead the church bells spell out Predestination, in slow and solemn strokes, as if they were keeping time with the march of all humanity towards the everlasting tomb. Gay? It is hardly the word.

Certainly, the passers-by show no signs of exuberant spirits. They walk without spring or speed. Visitors to Glasgow may hurry to get out of the rain, but the natives know they can't spend all their lives in sprinting practice, and so they walk quite slowly, but their heads are bent and averted and their faces appear to have lost definition, like statues too long weathered. A tram car comes lurching and squealing and grinding along, like a mechanized death-cart, and two or three figures materialize out of a close-mouth and climb silently on board. They had huddled together in the close without a word. Johnson once said that nobody could stand under the same shelter, out of the rain, with Burke and not know he was in the presence of a great man. If Burke had been a Glasgow man, which he nearly became, Johnson could have stood under the same shelter and never have known he was there.

Decidedly, the scene and the spirit of the people are far from gay, and a very large part of Glasgow is much like Eglinton Street. True, it is Sunday evening, which comes only once a week, but it rains practically all the time. Indeed, there are worse places than Eglinton Street. There is a place called Ark Lane, which looks as if it had been specially designed for the accommodation of lost souls. A walk along the whole of Dobie's Loan would make Mark Tapley throw up the sponge of cheerfulness.

For grime and gloom, Parliamentary Road and Cathedral Street are like Styx and Acheron running side by side. Garscube Road would make William Blake give back his bow and spear and chariot of fire and call it a day. Then, there is Florence Street, and College Street, and so on, and so on.

And yet, and yet . . . a couple of years ago, I attended a penitential affair called a dinner dance, in a London hotel. The guests were firmly requested not to sing to the music of the band. They observed this instruction so faithfully that very few of them showed any inclination even to dance. All went merry as a passing bell, until the band struck up "I belong to Glasgow". Almost on the instant the dance floor was crowded with vigorously whirling couples and everybody was singing, including the band.

What did the trick? It was hardly the song. The words are good, but there are better. The music is goodish, but there is much better. No, it was Glasgow itself, or rather the Glasgow Man filled with common humanity and the largest quantity of alcohol that his money can buy. He is aware of a strange ringing in the ears and a blurring of vision that often come upon him round about closing time, but though he is slightly uncertain in some of his sensory responses he is confident and serene. He is not in the least like the Little Man of Cockney cartoons who mildly complains that the world is pushing him around. The Glasgow Man is mildly reproachful because the world is pushing itself around. But the world is a good place, if it would only stay still—— It is a particularly good place if you happen to live in Glasgow. That is the theme song, and he has got half the world singing it.

Yes, there *is* something special about Glasgow. Imagine a song called "I belong to Bradford". If you can imagine it, there is only one thing to say about you. You come from Bradford.

CHAPTER TWO

THE PLACE

THE first visual impression of Glasgow is compactness. That is what strikes the visitor who does a little exploration. Walking or driving through the tenement streets, he is apt to get the feeling that the people of Glasgow live shoulder to shoulder and on top of each other. Open spaces are few, and, in most of the city, the continuous rows of tenements are broken only by an occasional unexplained piece of waste ground, that has the abrupt, unexpected effect of a missing tooth. For the rest, it is one tenement and then another, all of the same height and length and of the same severe design. Some are in grey stone and some in red, but outside of the residential areas, they all look the same. They are as close together as can be.

Seen from the air, Glasgow looks as tight as a fist, and it is possible to see that the general lay-out is far superior to the average. Glasgow looks very well from the air. It can all be taken in at a glance, and it has the attractiveness of a neat and elaborate scale-model. The neat, compact effect was much more obvious thirty-odd years ago, before the beginning of municipal housing estates. Unlike most cities Glasgow did not peter out in smaller and smaller houses, with villas followed by bungalows and semi-detached villas and isolated spots of new building. Glasgow just stopped. You knew to a yard when you were in and when you were out.

That was true, even of the suburban sectors of the perimeter, and it was strikingly evident in the sectors where working-class tenements met the fields like headland cliffs standing against the sea. (This is a slight exaggeration, for there was usually a grassless foreshore, littered with odd bricks and bits of broken masonry.) If a stranger, quite ignorant of its history, had visited Glasgow in 1917, he might easily have assumed that the city was still contained within the limits of fortifications only recently demolished. There was no amorphous fringe, no Greater Glasgow, nothing that could be called a "conurbation". Glasgow began smack at one point and finished smack at another. There was much to be said against the shape of Glasgow, but at least it was emphatic.

There are still relics of this sharp definition, notably in one part of the East End where the long tenements climb uphill and stop abruptly, like soldiers halting in line, but housing estates (or Schemes as they are always called) now mask the firm outline in many places. Take Great Western Road, for example. This road goes up and down with a fine, exhilarating swoop from the corner of Byres Road to Anniesland Cross. It is flanked on either side for almost all the way by open spaces and expensive villas, but it ends surprisingly in a double row of very good quality tenement buildings that would look more appropriate near the centre of a town. When the tenements stopped, Glasgow formerly stopped—stopped dead and for good, like a man getting off a bicycle. A brisk walker could pass the tenements and push over the fields ahead without passing another house till he came to Loch Lomond. Now, Anniesland Cross only marks the beginning of Knightswood, a municipal Housing Scheme with a larger population than Perth.

The same thing has happened at many other points of the perimeter. It is still possible to walk uphill from Rutherglen and behind Cathkin Braes to Carmunnock without noticing any great change in the wooded and pastoral landscape of thirty years ago, but the walk from Glasgow itself leads through a litter of villas. A generation ago, Carmunnock was a pleasant old stone village, perched on a steep hill and approachable only by foot. There was the peace and the solitude of the country in its few quiet streets. But now it is only a small speck in a "conurbation".

Yet in spite of the amorphous fringe, the hard core of Glasgow is as definite as before. The high tenements meet the new villas as uncompromisingly as they formerly met the fields. The old clash of city street and country has been replaced by a new clash of city street and suburban road. It is not so surprising, but it is quite as sharp. Glasgow is like a strong man who has put on a good deal of superficial fat. His outline has lost some of its definition but if you feel his arms, the hard and firm muscle is still there.

There has been little change of general appearance of the city proper for many years, except that, since the end of the Second War, some of the odd, disconcerting gaps between the tenements have been filled with pre-fabs. Cowering between the high buildings, they have a sad, boycotted look like chickens who are waiting in vain for the mother hen to open her wings and take them in. There has been some new building though not a great deal, and most of it is in decent harmony with the old. In such a characteristic stretch as the run from Dalmarnock Bridge through Bridgeton Cross to Glasgow Cross it is hard to think of any notable alteration in thirty years, or even fifty. If a man of Campbell-Bannerman's generation re-visited Glasgow from the grave, he would find it much less changed than he had anticipated.

It has been said that Glasgow looks well-planned from the air. The business part, at least, looks equally well-planned from the ground. That part starts at its Eastern end as a rectangle, but it bulges on the North side to take in part of Sauchiehall Street. Within a quite small area are the Municipal Buildings, the G.P.O., two of the principal railway stations, nearly all the headquarters of the big firms and the banks, most of the big hotels, the most popular and the most expensive shopping centres and even the principal clubs. It is a neat and valuable parcel.

Considering that a large part of the business area has been built over the shoulder of a quite considerable hill, the lay-out is surprisingly regular and convenient. Apart from the narrowness of some of the streets, it would be hard to find fault with the general design. There are particular blots, of course. The old Caledonian Railway should never have been permitted to extend their Central Station in the air across Argyle Street. Somebody slipped up when that was allowed or, at any rate, somebody was pushed. There are grave faults of proportion in George Square. The Scott pillar is ridiculously high, and the Cenotaph is badly placed and painfully squat.

Queen Street Station is both badly placed and badly built. Seen from the outside it has a dejected and temporary look, as if an enterprising company had run it up for an Exhibition and forgotten to pull it down again. Inside, it is dark and dreary and furnished with an indicator board as modern in design and conception as *The Rocket*. The Station opens at once into a steep and gloomy tunnel, perpetually filled with billowing smoke clouds. This tunnel has never been known to raise the holiday spirits of travellers, but it has killed a few. The gradient is sharp, and heavy trains require an extra engine to pull them out. There is a low-level station under the ground in Queen Street. It looks like hell on a wet day. It may be worth mentioning, that, as an extra amenity, the Luggage Office in Queen Street Station is in the open air.

The Central Station is a very different affair. It is clear and clean and has an air of space. All the main offices can be seen at a glance and the indicator can be read without calling on the assistance of the Station-master. The Men's Lavatory which runs underground right across the Station fills many a Glasgow man with modest pride. For nobility of proportion and fine functional adaptation, it has no parallel in this specialized form of interior architecture in the whole of the British Isles.

The most massive building in the area is the Municipal Buildings, but it is not the most happily conceived. With its deeply recessed windows sheltered by heavy stone eyebrows, it might have a certain functional attractiveness in a city where protection from the merciless glare of the sun is a primary consideration. But, in Glasgow, this is not even a secondary consideration. I once heard a story that Ruskin burst out laughing when he first saw this building. If he did, it was very unfair, for, if it had not been for Ruskin and people like him, Glasgow might have built something more sensible. In fact, Glasgow did build something more sensible in the modern addition at the back. Considering that the architects had to find some degree of harmony with the original building, it may be said that they did as well as could be expected.

On the other side of George Street from the Muncipal Buildings, and just outside the business area, is the Royal Technical College. (Until recently, the immediately surrounding area was one of the most spectacular examples of slum overcrowding in Europe. Balmano Brae on a Saturday night was worth going far to see.) As the College was built on and into the side of a very steep hill, it must have been an expensive job. It is said to be the largest single building devoted to education in the whole of Britain.

This may well be so, but the size is the only recommendation the building has. It is much too heavy for its purpose and there is a dark air about it. Of course, it is possible that the gloom is not so much architectural as functional. Generation after generation of engineering apprentices have gone to night school there to learn engineering drawing and other illiberal arts. Worn out after a day of physical work in the yards, kicking a paper ball about, boiling cans, playing nap and dodging the foreman, they had to change and wash and come out into the wet night to apply their minds to sterile mental labour. Other boys of the same age were having a glorious time in dance halls and billiards rooms and fish and chip shops, but the industrious apprentice had to waste the golden hours of youth over ruler and protractor and drawing board. No wonder the "Tech" looks like a great Minotaur in red standstone.

Apart from a few buildings which are unfortunately

designed and unfortunately large, the centre of Glasgow is decent and dignified. It may be admitted that the material helps a good deal, for a building of good stone has to try pretty hard to be really ugly. Apart from the glazed white of the Anchor Line building, the colour note of the area is a weathered and partly blackened grey. With few exceptions, the designs are simple and sufficient, and some of them are graceful. There is nothing that is vigorously offensive, nothing that painfully rubs the eye-balls like, for example, the Prudential building in Holborn.

Gordon Street succeeds in being a good street, without any assistance from the front of the Central Station. From St. Vincent Street downwards, Buchanan Street is as handsome a shopping centre as one could reasonably ask for, though the part above St. Vincent Street is shabby and nondescript enough. Eastwards from the lower end of Buchanan Street is a district mostly composed of warehouses and unobtrusive shops and offices, where it is easy to recall the past, Victorian and more remote. There are one or two old-fashioned and very pleasant pubs (the Cramond for example) where it would cause no surprise if the next customer to come in was wearing a frockcoat and side-whiskers and had some judicious observations to make on President Kruger. Quiet Virginia Street and still quieter Antigua Place recall the days of easy money, long since spent.

Ingram Street runs all the length of this quiet part. It has a tea-room designed by Charles Rennie MacIntosh a long lifetime ago which set a new standard for the whole country in the design and decoration of such harmless establishments. Near the far end of Ingram Street is the

Ramshorn Kirk and its dejected graveyard. In that graveyard lies L'Angelier who died untimely because he misunderstood the beautiful and talented Miss Madeleine Smith, one of the most remarkable women Glasgow or any other city has ever produced. West of the backwater area, there is an oblong bounded by St. Vincent Street and Argyle Street, Buchanan Street and Renfield Street. It is narrow but fairly deep and contains the offices of some of the most important firms.

At Renfield Street, the business centre begins to have serious trouble with the hill. In fact, until the coming of electric and motor transport, people thought Renfield Street had no big commercial future because of the steepness of its gradient. But now, Renfield Street is very important and increasingly so.

Across Renfield Street, St. Vincent Street, George Street and Bath Street take the shoulder of the hill and rise till they meet the skyline. They are all good streets in a close, unassertive Scottish manner, and the big houses have become business premises with very little outward change. The best of these streets is Bath Street, which has a little more of a continuous style than the others. There is an occasional evening in Glasgow when there is a hint of blue in the air. It is attractive and unusual, and on such an evening Bath Street looks more than well.

But the most remarkable building in this district is undoubtedly the large church which stands near the crown of St. Vincent Street. It has a commanding situation and is commanding in itself. It was built by an architect with a great local reputation, who is always known as "Greek" Thomson, but he might as well be known as "Egyptian" or "Assyrian" Thomson if his name is meant to indicate his style. The church is certainly interesting and unusual, but it is difficult to see its relevance to the Shorter Catechism and the Confession of Faith. However, the Free Kirk in the nineteenth century was liberal in everything except theology and fun, and "Greek" Thomson was given his head not only here but in two other churches, of which, I think, the one in Caledonia Road was by far his best, if only because it looks faintly like a church.

Thomson was undoubtedly a man of bold and considerable talent, but as a church builder he appears to have suffered from the dimness of his apprehension of what the building was intended for, and as a domestic architect, he could not conceive that a window ever was, or could be, anything more than just a hole in a wall.

North and south of these steep streets are two that have an easier way to make in the world. Bothwell Street curls round the base of the hill and was intended to be a very important thoroughfare, joining the centre of the city to the West End, but for some mysterious reason, it never came to life. Architecturally, it is a rag-bag of a street. There is a good modern office block, and opposite is the Y.M.C.A., which tries to make up in size for what it lacks in everything else. There is also a monumental mason's yard below street level where you can select some tombstones as you travel past by tram, and there is a good deal of ground occupied by nothing in particular. That is really all there is to say about Bothwell Street. Somebody had "vision" when Bothwell Street was planned. When there is no vision the people perish, but when there are no people the vision perishes. That is what has happened to Bothwell Street, but perhaps its time will come.

Sauchiehall Street enjoys an almost world-wide fame, which can only be explained on the theory that outsiders find the name peculiar in an interesting kind of way. When you mention that it is rather a wide street, you have exhausted its architectural merits. It is a street of high-quality shops, but it makes no attempt at cohesion of design and it contains several buildings which can only be described as horrible. Its proletarian sister, Argyle Street, is not wide, but it is long. The newer buildings have a blatant but honest vulgarity, and the survivals from the Victorian age have a quaint and wistful charm. Between Argyle Street and the river, there is a rather pleasant eighteenth-century church, and a small but beautiful tower. The river front is not attractive, and over the water begins the dreary waste of the industrial South Side.

The residential West End, behind and to the west of the pretty Kelvingrove Park, has some very pleasant little corners, and nearly all the houses stand in the intrinsic dignity of good stone, but undoubtedly the most attractive part of Glasgow is the suburb of Pollokshields. It is well wooded, which is refreshing in a city that is scandalously short of trees, and the big, solid grey stone houses are both pleasant and impressive.

There are not many remarkable buildings in Glasgow. The ancient Cathedral is nearly dwarfed by the gross and bullying bulk of the Royal Infirmary but the crypt is very fine. The main University building is rather sad to look on, but some of the additions have merit. Decent dignity is the best that can be claimed for the business and residential areas, and no one would dare to claim either decency or dignity for the working-class areas. Yet, although there is gloom and grime in wholesale quantities, there is not the shabby meanness of those dreary rows of huddled little smoke-blackened brick houses which disfigure most English industrial towns. Glasgow is not beautiful, but neither is it shoddy.

CHAPTER THREE

THE PEOPLE

G LASGOW is a heavily overcrowded and heavily industrialized city with an exceedingly mixed population. These fundamental facts go far to explain the
Glasgow character, which is at once cosmopolitan and
provincial. A working-class woman who had moved from
Partick in Glasgow to Finsbury Park in London, worked
for two years as a carriage-cleaner in King's Cross Station
before she decided in a spirit of enterprising inquiry to
take a bus into the heart of London to see the sights. She
saw St. Paul's and Parliament, Whitehall and the Abbey,
and decided that once was enough. She told me there was
nothing in London to impress anyone who had seen the
Municipal Buildings in George Square. (I was surprised
that she found anything to equal Partick Burgh Hall.)
She then showed me snaps of her nephew's bungalow in
Abadan. In her lack of intermediate vision, she was a
typical native of Glasgow.

The provinciality of Glasgow is partly explained by its
distance from London and its lack of tourist attractions.
There is, of course, a very heavy train and even aeroplane
traffic between the cities, but the visitors from London
are nearly all travelling on business. It is true that some
of the regular visitors have developed a strong affection
for Glasgow and have come to understand that it is in
many ways a more interesting city than Edinburgh, but
they have conspicuously failed to persuade their English

friends to come and find out for themselves. A large proportion of the English who travel to Perth every year for the Twelfth or who patronize Saint Andrews and North Berwick or the Edinburgh Festival never think of calling in at Glasgow, even to change trains.

The Scotland these people know is what they like to regard as the "real" Scotland, Princes Street and Murrayfield, the Old Course and Braemar Games, the grouse-moors and salmon rivers. They are aware of Glasgow as a vigorous and richly humorous place, but they regard it as an alien growth, as something foreign to the authentic Scotland of the Waverley Novels and *The Tatler*.

As they know nothing about Glasgow, the people of Glasgow are firmly determined to know nothing about them. This is perhaps a pity, for the tourists are not altogether wrong. Glasgow is indeed partly an alien growth, and the inhabitants who can claim pure Lowland descent are decidedly in the minority.

It could not well be otherwise. From the end of the eighteenth century to the end of the nineteenth century, the population of Glasgow rose dizzily. In 1901 the population was ten times the census figure of 1801. This increase was achieved partly by absorbing neighbouring townships and partly by attracting workers from the surrounding countryside, but these were minor causes.

The major cause was immigration from afar. The Highlands provided large numbers who did a good deal to dilute the Lowland atmosphere. They were not completely at home and they were not entirely welcome. Pre-industrial Glasgow was the capital of the Whigamores. The douce citizens of the small but prosperous mercantile town lived altogether too near the Highlanders to like them. (Gaelic was spoken within easy walking distance of Glasgow Cross.) If Baillie Nicol Jarvie was rather a caricature of a Glasgow merchant in his general outlook, his attitude towards the Highlanders was quite representative. The men of Glasgow did not like Highland manners or Highland morals, Highland politics or Highland religion.

Edinburgh rejected a statue of King William, liquidator of the MacDonalds of Glencoe, but Glasgow accepted it. Edinburgh was horrified by the butchery of Culloden. Glasgow University gave the Butcher an honorary degree. Edinburgh was in two minds about Bonnie Prince Charlie, but Glasgow was in one mind. Glasgow wanted to see the last of him as cheaply and as quickly as possible.

The divergence of political and economic interest between Highlands and Lowlands is no longer of serious importance (though it might become sharp again under Home Rule), but the divergence of temperament remains. That is why the feeling between the Highlander and the Western Lowlander is something like the feeling between the Welshman and the Southern Englishman. There is one Glasgow man who always adds a note of caution and explanation to his name whenever he makes a new acquaintance. "My name is McLeod," he says carefully, "but I am a Lowland McLeod." He is not alone among Glasgow men in regarding Highlanders as something less than spiritual twins.

It would be foolish to exaggerate the difference between Highlands and Lowlands, but History still whispers its warnings and reproaches in the unconscious ear, and the sympathy is certainly not complete. There is some uneasiness in personal relationship, which is indicated by a tendency of Highlanders, even of Highland students, to huddle together, and to indulge occasionally in back-scratching and wire-pulling, to a degree which greatly annoys the Lowlanders who are highly proficient at these exercises themselves. It must be added that the high proportion of Highlanders in the Police force does not make the Glasgow working man think any more kindly of the Gael.

There is no means of knowing, even roughly, how many Highlanders there are in Glasgow, but they are a notable element in the population. Jokes about (and against) Highlanders are readily appreciated in music-halls and pantomimes. The Highlanders' Institute is well-known, and Clan Societies flourish as heartily as they do in London. The railway bridge over Argyle Street is known as "The Highlanders' Umbrella", there are Highland pubs, and there are streets where the hard Lowland tongue sounds strangely among soft exile voices that recall the rainy glens and the lonely islands, Uist and Barra and Mull, and the towering crags of Skye.

Much more alien and much more numerous has been the incursion from Ireland. This, indeed, is Glasgow's favourite problem, and it is one of long standing. One hundred and fifty years ago, there were loud squawks and more measured and serious declamations on the apparently inexhaustible flood of Irish who landed bare-footed, hungry and most unfairly muscular to do more work for less money than the natives felt was consistent with the inalienable Rights of Man.

For longer than anyone can remember, the population of Glasgow has been at least one-fifth "Irish", but "Irish" is a word that demands severe qualification. Sometimes the "Irish" are referred to as "Southern Irish", regardless of the fact that if they are Irish at all, they almost all come from the North. But "Southern Irish" in Glasgow, is a polite synonym for Catholic Irish, while "Northern Irish" is a synonym for Protestant Irish.

The proportion of "Southern Irish" has never been so high as in the present generation. Almost one-third of Glasgow's schoolchildren are in Catholic Schools. (There are several considerable towns in the neighbourhood where the percentage touches fifty.) But these children are only to be called Irish in the local and technical sense. Few of them have ever seen Ireland and many are of the third and fourth generation of settlers. Many more are of thoroughly mixed parentage, for there has long been a large though generally unnoticed admixture of the races by marriage. In some Catholic parishes, half the marriages are "mixed". This, of course, means a marriage of mixed religions, but a glance at any Catholic school register would soon show that a mixture of religion nearly always means a mixture of race as well. The mixture does not always result in a gain for Catholic schools. There are many allegedly "pure" Scots in Glasgow who never refer to the Irish in their ancestry and perhaps are unaware of it, but the Protestant Boyles and Kellys and Shannons can hardly imagine that all their forefathers signed the National Covenant.

The "Northern" Irish are a smaller, but still formidable body, though the most active propagandists of the Irish Problem have always been careful not to inquire how many of them there are. There are constituencies in Glasgow where a solid Orange vote can always be guaranteed to save the Conservative deposit. The large population of Irish Protestants or their descendants make Glasgow one of the few towns where a really good Orange Walk could be staged until the police decided that enough was a good deal more than a feast, and told the Orangemen to walk elsewhere.

There is a good deal of come-and-go between Glasgow and Belfast, particularly among the shipbuilding workers, and there are simple-minded men in Belfast who look on Toronto as the Second City of the Empire and Glasgow as the First, London being the sink of iniquity where Ulster is constantly in danger of betrayal.

It may be said that if the Irish Protestant or Orange element is tactfully ignored in public pronouncements, that is not through any modest self-effacement. If the Orangemen make no noise in the Press, they make quite a deal in the streets from time to time. The most common complaint of the Glasgow police against turbulent citizens is the singing of "party songs". Sometimes, it is "Kevin Barry" that gives offence, and at other times it is "Boyne Water". When both are sung together, the police have more than singing to complain about.

The English were later arrivals, at least in any strength, but considerable numbers have settled in Glasgow since the end of the first World War. They have settled down so unobtrusively and fitted in so easily that they have been almost entirely unnoticed. This might be ascribed to tact, except that the Glasgow man is constantly appalled by the English lack of tact. It might be truer to say that the English have settled down without fuss because they are not a fussy people, and are beautifully free from the exile complex. The Englishman on his own side of the Border can smile with kindly amusement at the alcoholic nostalgia of the Clan gatherings and the Burns Dinners, but the Englishman on the Scottish side of the Border has no intention of providing kindly amusement for anybody else. This is much to his credit, but at the same time it must be said that there are some Englishmen, and more Englishwomen, who make themselves at home in Glasgow as a bossy district visitor makes herself at home in the house of a humble client. To hear their conversation and to watch their behaviour is to begin to understand why Pandit Nehru is what he is.

In the Lanarkshire mining towns, which are grimy satellites of the Glasgow, Poles and Lithuanians are to be found in fair numbers. (In at least one pub "Gentlemen" is painted above the lavatory door in what I take to be Lithuanian.) In Glasgow itself, there are Smiths and Spences whose fathers had East-European names that did not stand sea travel.

The Italians are much more prominent than their numbers would justify. They have nearly a monopoly of the ice-cream and fish-and-chips shop trades, and they performed a very real social service by refusing to be intimidated by the inspissated Sabbatarianism which thoroughly cowed the native Scot fifty years ago, and cows him to some extent, even to-day. The Scot who most sullenly resented the tyranny of a Hebraic Sabbath resented something which had meaning to him and which was residuary within himself. But the Italian showed his white teeth and laughed. To him, the thing was so silly that it could not be serious. He sold his ice-cream in cheerful defiance of a convention that seemed to him as foreign as something from Tibet, all unaware that a century before, the most daring Radicals skulked across

Glasgow Green on a Sunday, clear of the Burgh boundary, to eat curds and whey in Rutherglen.

The first generation of Italians mostly learn English imperfectly and with difficulty, while some of the women never learn it at all, but their sons become merged and assimilated with remarkable fullness and finality. Indeed, the richest and most painful Glasgow speech can often be heard from the lips of an Italian whose father's native speech is Neapolitan, equally rich and perhaps equally painful. The Italians are enterprising, industrious and friendly. They are almost universally popular. They have qualities of vigorous and uninhibited enjoyment, which are much appreciated by the Lowland Scots, not because they lack these qualities themselves, but because they lack the ability to express them, except in a seasonal and unduly sensational way.

There are, of course, Jews in Glasgow. The majority who are poor mostly live in and around the Gorbals, while the prosperous Jews tend to cluster together in certain residential areas from which, also, the Gentiles tend to move out. Everywhere in Britain the local estimate of Jewish influence in business and on public affairs is grossly exaggerated, but the Glasgow estimate is wilder than most. Glasgow Jews follow the familiar occupations of their race and some of them, including Sir Maurice Bloch, are prominent and respected citizens, but the fundamentals of Glasgow commercial and industrial life would scarcely be affected if all the Jews went away. Their contribution to academic life has not been notable, and the only one of them to reach national prominence in politics has been Emmanuel Shinwell, who is not wholly a Glasgow man. If any Glasgow man can find local evi-

"DOON THE WATTER"

dence to support his belief in the Protocols of the Elders of Zion, his imagination is stronger than his reasoning powers. Another Glasgow man would say "he ought to have his head looked"; there would be nothing inside.

A half-crazy local prophet called The Clincher used to declare that all the real Scots in Glasgow could be accommodated in one tramcar. Even as a piece of rhetoric, this was an undue over-statement, for, in fact, the "real" Scots do quite firmly dominate almost every element of the city's life. The heads of companies, the outstanding men of learning and technique and the arts, the administrators and leaders of opinion and the uncomplicated, undistinguished men of the simple, satisfactory money bags are "real" Scots in an overwhelming majority. In quality, they are dominant.

Yet, if the "real" Scots tried to round up all the others and run them out of the town, they would find themselves rather heavily out-numbered. Some of them are distressed by this thought, but with insufficient reason. Glasgow has been a strikingly successful melting-pot in creating a common character, if not a common theology or ideology.

In June of 1940, a young Glasgow Italian was greatly distressed because his father had been put in prison, as a first step towards internment. He had an interview with his father in prison and then closely questioned the broadspoken typically Glasgow sentry at the gate about possible anti-Italian prejudice. At first the sentry gave evasive and curt answers, and then, under persistent and detailed questioning, he became impatient and irritated. At last, he could stand no more.

"Ask me my name," he said, in his richest Glasgow.

"What's your name got to do with it?" the worried young man asked, in natural surprise.

"Ask me," said the soldier stubbornly.

"Well, what is it?"

"Guidicci."

The worried young man was soon in the Army himself, where everybody, from the Colonel downwards, called him by his first name. He was exceedingly popular. He had something.

He was a Glasgow man.

CHAPTER FOUR

THE GLASGOW MAN

THE characteristic Glasgow man who has been formed from a mixture and a partial mingling of races is not among the most beautiful of God's creatures. The better-looking of the middle class are a tall, powerful and vigorous lot, well built for Rugby and hiking and perhaps mountaineering in youth, and it is regrettable that many young men of excellent muscle and muscular co-ordination take to golf at an age when they should still be playing real games. These men carry the years uncommonly well. Few of them grow paunchy, and the combination of white hair and a soldierly straight back is common enough among Glasgow men who have spent all their lives in sedentary work. They eat and are not notably sparing of cordial liquors, but they live long and they live strong.

The three Stevenson brothers are an example of family longevity. The best known was Sir Daniel, who became Lord Provost of Glasgow and Chancellor of the University and made a large fortune by buying coal in Scotland and selling it in Spain. The rewards of this apparently simple operation enabled him to make academic and cultural endowments that were impressive enough, even by American standards. Modern languages, music and a curious moralistic discipline called Citizenship were all beneficiaries of his large generosity. He was a man of culture who had a remarkable collection of friends, or at least acquaintances, in high places, including President Wilson, a string of French statesmen and a German called Hitler. He was the main support of the Scottish Ambulance which had such a controversial history in Spain, and he died full of years and honours at the age of ninety-two.

A brother of Sir Daniel who was also prominent in industry, though not in Glasgow, made an even larger fortune and lived, I think, rather longer, and yet another brother devoted himself to painting with much distinction. Macaulay Stevenson also made many friends among the famous, and at the time of writing he is still happily among us, at the hearty age of ninety-eight.*

The best demonstration of lasting strength I ever saw was given by a junior member of one of the most famous industrial families in the West of Scotland. When I met this gentleman he was dressed in such a sombre and uncompromisingly Victorian way that it would have been no surprise if he had produced a Temperance tract from his frock coat pocket. Instead, he produced a piece of chalk and slipped his little finger inside the ring of a fifty-six pound weight. He then lifted the weight up on his finger and wrote his name, with the chalk, on the wall. He was over sixty at the time.

Such men are exceptional, but the average Glasgow middle-class man is a sufficiently tough specimen. The facial type is one of high and prominent bone. It is a type that weathers exceedingly well, and such men grow handsomer as they grow older. The men with the more prominently marked features may look a little bleakly aggressive in youth and maturity, but they fine down with the years, and gain distinction without losing definition.

*Alas, since writing, dead.

At any age, flabby faces are as scarce in Glasgow as flabby bellies. The Glasgow merchants of to-day are a leaner and less highly coloured lot than the men that Raeburn painted.

If the middle classes have shown some change over a century or two, the working classes have shown a bigger change in a single lifetime. Forty years ago, one of the most prominent proletarian types was locally known as the "wee bauchle", a man little over five feet with features that had been assembled in careless haste, and shambling legs that bore eloquent testimony to the lifelong effects of rickets. He looked as if a gentle push would send him on his back and rob him of the energy to get up again, and in the first World War many a big soldier from other parts allowed himself to be deceived by appearances. Many a public house row in Glasgow and Somewhere-in-France ended with the big soldier holding his jaw together and wondering what had hit him. The answer was simple. He had been hit by the wee bauchle's head. When the war-cry, "Gie him the crust" is heard, it is advisable for the largest adversary to remove himself to the greatest possible distance, in the shortest possible time.

The wee bauchle was, of course, the product of the grimmest slum conditions in Western Europe. Those who lived through a Cowcaddens or Gorbals childhood had a very high survival value. They were under-weight and undersized, but so was Jimmy Wilde, and they showed a capacity for enduring the unhealthiest conditions and the greatest discomforts which proved to be invaluable in more serious fighting than pub brawling.

The contrast between the slum-hardened proletarian and the artisan is fortunately not nearly so great as it used to be. Rickets have been virtually abolished, and there has been a considerable increase in weight, even in the worst districts. But the contrast is still there. The skilled men in heavy engineering and ship-building have always been a solid-looking lot, with heavy shoulders and massively strong hands. In fact, they have always been too well-fed and muscular to give much support to the political contention that the Iron Heel was trampling the life out of them. The hollow-cheeked Jimmy Maxton did give the impression that his next peroration might well be his last, but Jimmy Maxton was a University man and a school teacher by profession. The really representative spokesman of the workers was Mr. Davy Kirkwood, now Lord Kirkwood, who was, and is, a most striking example of the body-building virtues of porridge and Scotch broth. Whatever Capitalism may have denied to Mr. Kirkwood, it was certainly not a sufficiency of food.

The unskilled workers are still far enough behind the artisans and the middle class to be a different physical type, but the contrast in physique is very much greater than the contrast in temperament and habits. Glasgow is the most democratic city in Britain. This is a bold statement, but he would be a bold man who would deny it, unless, perhaps, he came from Dundee.

Glasgow is democratic in ways that are not only unknown but would be utterly incomprehensible anywhere in England. That is not to say that there are no snobs in Glasgow. There are, but they are known as snobs, and they know themselves as snobs. Social habits, differences and segregations that are taken as the law of Nature in England are considered to be snobbish and undesirable in Glasgow.

Glasgow is not ill-supplied with pubs which cater for

a wide range of income and social standards, but the number of saloon bars could be numbered on the fingers of one hand, and these have all some special justification. The best-known saloon bar is probably the one in the Grosvenor, opposite the Central Station, but the majority of the regular clients of the Grosvenor are totally indif-

"INTELLECTUAL PUB"

ferent as to whether they use the public or the saloon, and, in fact, use one or the other, as is convenient at the moment. If the ordinary Glasgow publican nourishes ambitions to make his place select, it never occurs to him to make two or three bars. He shuts out women instead.

There is one pub which is much frequented by the men and women of the B.B.C., and also by the coal-heavers of the district. They drink on the friendliest terms, and from time to time, the coal-heavers make useful comments on the programmes. It must be understood that there is nothing self-consciously democratic about this kind of mixing. The thing is taken simply and totally for granted. The man on your right may be a coal-heaver still unwashed and in his working clothes, while the man on your left may imagine he is a modern poet or may be, in fact, a wealthy ship-builder. Conversation will be general and very likely combative, and nobody, not even the coal heaver, will think there is anything queer about it. If you don't like it like that, you can do your drinking at home.

It is not suggested that this cheerful spirit of brotherhood should be imitated in England, or even that it could be. The Glasgow pub has two social advantages that are sadly denied to the English pub. These are a rough community of language and a rough community of interests.

The community of language is not complete. At one end of the scale, a consciously genteel section of the suburban *bourgeoisie* affect a mincing and artificial accent which is called "Keelvinside" by the derisive majority. (It is regrettable that Glasgow Academy, otherwise a most worthy school, inculcates a kind of utility version of this painful *patois*.) At the other end of the scale there is a slum dialect which can scarcely be called language at all. The medial and final "T" are never pronounced, and articulation does not exist. Shapeless words come slithering out in a slovenly mumble known as a "slush". Some of the most distinguished experts in communication by slush ought to make good ventriloquists, for they can indulge in the exercise they call speech without moving their lips at all.

But the essence of the slush is not an individual intonation or pronunciation, but plain barbaric laziness. When these folk take the trouble to pronounce words at all, they pronounce them very much the same as the great majority of Glasgow people. The common speech of Glasgow is aggressively unadorned, and there is no substantial difference between the speech of an intelligent worker and an educated professional man. One may be slightly broader and harsher than the other, but the pronunciation, accent and intonation are the same. If a Londoner who has risen to wealth from the proletarian condition wishes to have his origins forgotten, his greatest difficulty will undoubtedly be his speech. He will be a very clever man indeed if he can cauterize the Cockney completely out of his voice.

No Glasgow man has any such difficulty. If he wishes to talk "pan loaf" or "glass door" he will no doubt sound ridiculous, but no more so than those who were born to the pretentiousness of Keelvinside. But, if he merely wishes to talk the plain speech of educated and prosperous Glasgow men, he need do no more than remember that the letter "T" is not mute in any word.

Such differences as there are in the common speech have no social significance, and communication is uninhibited by shibboleths of class or culture. But the people who can talk together without embarrassment have also something to talk about. Conversation in English pubs, tea rooms and other places of accidental encounter is governed by a quiet determination to talk about nothing that might possibly lead to disagreement. As disagreement is very likely between people of different income and manners and social habits, it may be as well the social classes are kept, or keep themselves, apart. But the Glasgow man is burdened by no such delicacy. He likes nothing better than an argument and a head-on clash of ideas and principles. The working-man's zeal for controversy is undamped by any thought of his educational disadvantages, and the middle-class man is no more deterred by the thought that he might be lowering himself.

Glasgow working men will talk about religion, Communism, Socialism, Capitalism, the United States, football, boxing and the right way to treat Germany with religious zeal and theological dogmatism. There is no pub in Glasgow where the range of conversation is as limited as it is in the average London public bar. The current form of horses and racing dogs receives sufficient and respectful attention, but other issues which arouse an equal interest and pugnacity are freely and fully treated. In England (at least in the South), casual social intercourse is limited to middle-class and working-class trivialities, but in Glasgow there is always somebody ready to talk about something else. Good English conversation is almost invariably monologue, but good Glasgow conversation is a free-for-all.

The difference is partly to be explained by the deliberate English cultivation of social mildness. If an Englishman is accused by his fellows of creating "trouble and strife", he stands condemned. That is not to say that the English are empty of principle or passion. They will respect a man for feeling deeply or acting according to the exigencies of some lonely purpose, but they disapprove if he speaks out loud about it. The English social instinct aims to create the largest possible area where men of conflicting views may meet and talk about anything except their views. They are the world's worst missionaries. That may be why they proved to be the world's best Imperialists. An Englishman of my acquaintance told me a story of something trivial that had happened at a meeting where he took the chair. He was a member of the Liberal Party who made no bones about the fact that he was a High Tory in politics and in much else, but he took the chair at a meeting which had been called to found a new branch of the Labour Party. The local Labour zealots were conscious that they were not conversant with the rules of public assemblies, and they asked him to help them out, in a neighbourly way, and he would have thought very poorly of himself if he had been tempted to refuse. He explained all this in a casual and quite incidental way. It was not the point of the story he was telling. He did not realize that it was the point of the story of his race since the age of Addison. It explained why there is such profound social peace in England. It also explains why there is no conversation.

Nobody in Glasgow could regard his behaviour without intellectual and moral horror. In Glasgow controversy is still much alive, and you think none the worse of a man for believing that he is a political, social and religious scoundrel and saying so to his face. Curiously enough, this makes for ease in intercourse. The English are tongue-tethered by the limitations they impose upon their own range of talk. They are Bowdlerists who will say nothing that might cause embarrassment to the tenderest maiden mind. Glasgow men are Rabelaisians. Rabelaisianism has its own dangers, but dullness is not one of them.

The Scots are, all of them, a disputatious race, and their

natural tastes are easily satisfied in Glasgow where suitable subjects for dispute are exceedingly numerous. It is sometimes said that a long and bitter course of theological argument has formed the Scottish aptitude for argument in general, but this is a contention which is rather hard to sustain. The English have spent much more time than the Scots have ever done in arguing about religious doctrine. Since the final defeat of the Episcopal Church at the Glorious Revolution, there has been no considerable Dissent in Scotland on a matter of belief or even of practice. Presbyterianism has always split on some point of Church Government. The Scots are profoundly anti-Erastian. The English are Erastian. The Prayer Book Debate in the Commons, which was largely influenced by a Glasgow man, shocked the Scots, not because they had any opinion on the merits of the case, but because the case had been submitted to Parliament at all and they would have been solid in support of any church party which had defied the State authority. It was a representative Scot who said, "I have been out in every Secession since the U.P." He was a small shopkeeper with no vested interest in secessions, but he was plainly looking forward to one or two more before he died. Perhaps an Englishman would be shocked at him.

Argument about Church government has saddled Scotland with a religious literature of unparalleled unreadability, but it has trained the national aptitude and appetite for argument about anything at all. Not everybody can dispute on the subtleties of doctrine, but everybody can say something on the definite issues of the relations of Church and State. It is not necessary to believe in the Church, or even in the State, to hold views on such matters and to press them strongly at highly inconvenient and irrelevant times. The transfer of this argumentative principle from religion to politics is obviously very easy, and the change from Radicalism to the entirely contrary creed of Socialism was effected in Scotland with no difficulty at all. Scottish Socialists have always been more interested in context than in content. That explains why Scottish Socialism has produced so many solid and worthy politicians, but has never anywhere, at any time, produced from anybody anything remotely resembling an idea.

The sad but undeniable fact is not at all to be explained by lack of brains. In fact, Scottish talk, and particularly Glasgow talk, is better than English not merely because the Scots have much greater zest for a verbal up-and-downer, but also because they are, on the whole, more intelligent. This is a rash thing to say and the claim could not possibly be sustained against the upper-ranges of the English intellect, but if the man-in-the-Glasgow-street is conceivably no more clear-headed than the man-in-the-London-street, he can at least express himself with immensely greater relevancy and logic. An eloquent rabble-rouser who had soared above and away from the nominal subject of his discourse was once halted at a Glasgow meeting, by a large navvy who rose from his seat and called out "For God's sake" in a stricken voice and sat down again, having purged his soul.

A well-known philosopher once addressed a series of meetings in Glasgow University, and noted with great surprise that the questions he was asked were all on the subject of his lecture. But nobody else was surprised. The Glasgow people took ordinary relevance for granted, as the meagre minimum of rational discussion. It is, of course, a minimum. It is not much to say for anybody, but it cannot be said for everybody, and it can be said for the Glasgow man.

It cannot be expected that an almost totally democratic and a thoroughly disputatious community should be noted for the refinements of social courtesy. The public servants are frequently gruff in their approach, and relations between the public transport workers and the passengers are far from cordial. But the services are unusually efficient, and an abrupt, pugnacious attitude which takes the visitor aback neither annoys nor depresses the native. It is almost unknown for any Glasgow man to call another "Sir", and when Glasgow workmen invade a house it is also almost unknown that they should make any effort at all to avoid spreading dirt or any effort to clear up the mess they have made. On the other hand, their technical superiority is immeasurable. If a Glasgow workman is called in to stop a pipe from leaking, he stops that pipe from leaking. If he is asked to mend a window or fix a lock, the window is mended or the lock is fixed. This may seem incredible to those who are accustomed only to the pleasant-spoken Southern tradesmen who are politely anxious not to cause Ma'am any more trouble than they can help, and are still polite, pleasant and unruffled the fourth time they come round to do the same simple job.

The Glasgow man would by no means accept the finding that he does a better job with worse grace. The formal courtesies of the English epicures seem to him almost unendurably effeminate, but he also suspects the Englishman of insincerity. He believes that there is more human warmth and candid friendliness in Glasgow than in most

4

other places, and the verdict of hordes of soldiers of many nations during two World Wars gives him solid basis for the belief. He thinks there is something deeply and inhumanly wrong in the aloofness which marks class relations in England, and again he has a good case to make for himself. Yet, it must be conceded that he carries the rough diamond philosophy rather too far at times. A widespread habit of using foul language in public places without consideration for sex or age is not easily explained or excused. It is not pleasant to hear children of less than school age pattering obscenities for lack of any other vocabulary.

If the Glasgow man would not win the unstinted approval of Chesterfield or Castiglione, he is yet a worthy citizen, intelligent and serious-minded above the average and also above the average in human generosity and friendliness. He is well trained at his job, and might even be called industrious by the unexacting British standards. In all things, and at all times, he is democratic. There can be few cities in the world where people get on so well without the guidance or example of any kind of aristocracy. There is no aristocracy of birth or race or wealth or fashion.

"The only pedigrees in Glasgow are in the Dog Show." This not very sparkling aphorism from a Scottish play brought the house down in Glasgow night after night. It was welcomed and approved as the statement of a great and worthy truth.

But the absence of an aristocracy has its disadvantages. Much may be said against the aristocrat, and it has been said with enthusiasm on many occasions, but he has his uses. Sometimes, though not always, he sets a high standard of probity in public life, and he may be very effective in leading and forming public æsthetic taste and in refining social converse and customs. If the aristocrat's record of public service is rather patchy in these matters, he is much more consistent in setting an example of defiance of sour and censorious respectability. Many an aristocrat has helped himself lavishly from the public funds and has been a self-assured Philistine in art, but very few of them have ever been intimidated by the frown of Stiggins or Podsnap or Holy Willie. The earnest prodding finger and the sharp word out of season are wasted on those who have a bland conviction that their function in life is to lead, not to follow.

But the people of Glasgow, for all their pugnacity and fondness for dispute, are much awed by the claims of respectability and are distinctly sheepish in their attitude towards moral improvers. The inheritance of Puritanism is still heavy upon them. The upholders of Sabbath Observance have had to yield a good deal of ground in the present century, but not nearly so much as might have been expected from the change in public opinion, and the Glasgow Sunday is still deeply dismal without even any consistency in its prohibitions. The Sabbatarians who believe that they are fulfilling an imperative religious duty are not to be blamed if they are stubborn in defence of their faith, but some blame must attach to the majority who accept so large a measure of interference in their private affairs when they no longer profess the faintest belief in the faith which justifies the interference. Puritanism has lasted much better than Presbyterianism. It is a powerful force, even in the Labour Movement, where there are men quite ready to declare their atheism but are very wary in approving of Sunday cinemas or sport.

The lack of courage and full conviction in the cakes-and-ale brigade is the reason why the Glasgow pub is not only strikingly democratic but is also uncommonly dingy. Temperance has successfully blocked every attempt to humanize and liberalize the pub. Music and food are unknown, and games nearly so. Temperance has fought to make drinking naked and ashamed, and has succeeded, because those who are condemned to discomfort and sometimes to positive dirt are mostly afraid to fight back.

What makes them afraid is a lack of inner confidence, which is itself caused by a lack of full inner conviction. Many Glasgow men have spent a large part of their lives in areas where Puritanism is not even a word, but few of them get Puritanism completely out of their systems. They may resent and condemn it, but they are resenting and condemning something which can still stir an unacknowledged self-reproach. It may be that all democratic societies are especially subject to pressure through organized minority groups, and the Glasgow community certainly is. That is one of the reasons why Glasgow men admire Burns so deeply, and even more as a man than as a poet. He challenged the oppressive convention of his day with total self-assurance. He reinforced defiance with disdain. But Burns, of course, was a highly unusual man. He was his own aristocracy. One could wish that Glasgow had a few men like Burns to-day, though it would be desirable if they did not give hostages to fortune in such a wholesale way.

Another excellent Glasgow quality which is perhaps overdone is a strong dislike of pretentiousness in any form. The Glasgow man is exceedingly quick to discover the faintest indication of "side" and nothing gives him greater pleasure than to take down the offender. Lifemanship is a game which Glasgow people do not think funny at all. Any kind of affectation is disliked and decried. In work and social habits and fashions and in intellectual activity, Glasgow values the homespun qualities and no other. The man who tries to have himself valued in any respect for rather more than he is runs a great danger of being valued for much less than he is. Glasgow is not ready to believe that a man may be affected and yet have very solid and even brilliant qualities, or that a bit of an exhibitionist may really have something to exhibit. This scepticism sometimes leads to a serious under-rating of unusual persons. When Algernon Charles Swinburne spent some weeks roaming about Glasgow University the students were inclined to laugh at his exceedingly fancy dress. It did not occur to them that they themselves were much more fancily dressed, for they all wore a picturesque gown of glaring red. The gown was uniform, and therefore it was as unpretentious as the business man's bowler of to-day.

If Glasgow sometimes under-values the fancy dress qualities, it sometimes over-values the homespun variety. Many a Glasgow citizen is highly respected because he is wholly unnoticeable. He does his job and never has much to say for himself. It is not suspected that he does not have much to say for himself because there is little that he could say, and that he does not show off for the good reason that he has nothing to show. So long as he is quietly unassertive, except of course in argument, it is presumed that there are sound and solid qualities hidden in him somewhere.

Dislike of pretentiousness leads to an acceptance of uniformity, and that, in turn, to an over-valuing of mediocrity. Glasgow is honest, intelligent, good-hearted and friendly, but stubbornly set against all kinds of flash or display. As a result, Glasgow is at times a trifle dull. It is not the Glasgow man's instinct to be dull, but he respects a remarkable number of taboos, except for spectacular outbursts at consecrated seasons, and not the least powerful of his taboos is the taboo against nonsense. A little bit of nonsense might do him a great deal of good.

CHAPTER FIVE

THE GLASGOW WOMAN

THE influence of Glasgow women on social life and habits is much less than the influences of their fair sisters in, say, Edinburgh or London. The reason is not far to seek. Glasgow is predominantly a proletarian city and it is in middle-class circles that the much advertised soothing and refining qualities of women have their fullest and freest play.

Women exert most of their influence through marriage, and in the working class group the husband is very much the head of the family. The wife talks about her "man" as, in Dickens's time, she might have talked about her "master", and she means very much the same thing. That is not to say that the habit of deference is universal. There are some working-class women who dominate the household, and many who are ever ready with a caustic tongue, but the great majority take it for granted and without question that the husband is the boss. More often than not he never thinks of telling his wife what he earns and she as seldom thinks of asking. There is a pleasing primitive simplicity about this conception of marriage and in many respects it works out very well. But it does very severely limit the influence that the wives can exercise on social life.

One Glasgow man, home on leave from the Army, confided to a friend that he had been compelled to fetch his wife a weighty clump on the ear. He was not a man of domineering nature or of rash brutality, but he felt that some emphatic action was demanded when he found his wife reading a book. Not a newspaper, mark you, but a real book, with covers. This had to be stopped by the simplest and most direct method.

It is not suggested that the behaviour of this soldier from the wars returning was entirely typical. There are many working-class husbands who can see their wives reading a book without being overcome with a feeling of incredulous horror. There are many who even read books themselves. But the soldier was typical enough in one thing. He took it for granted, as a law of Nature, that the culture and conduct of the home would be decided by himself, and that his decision would be accepted without question. Some nattering might be tolerated in an easy-going, masculine way, but defiance on a serious matter like reading books must be immediately suppressed and punished.

Most working class women accept this attitude with more or less philosophy. They take it for granted that if they have any opinions at all on matters outside the home they must be the husband's opinions, and they would consider it an act of disloyalty to cast their vote in a different direction. In the proletarian world, women are an immensely important but an immensely passive element. The wife may nourish dreams of spreading a cloth on the table, or even putting some flowers in a vase, but she would do nothing of the kind against the frown of her "man".

Because of this submissiveness on the part of working-class women, the social atmosphere of Glasgow is largely masculine, and the forms of chivalry are not much regarded. Hats are not readily raised, seats are not readily surrendered. Indeed, the behaviour of the Glasgow man in a predominantly masculine gathering like a football match leaves almost everything to be desired. Aversion to nonsense of any kind prohibits any delicate deference to feminine whims.

As a result, the manners of Glasgow children are bad. It may be surmised that they would be better if women exercised a greater authority, but the sad fact remains. The bad manners are not positive. That is to say, the passing stranger is no more likely to be incommoded or insulted in Glasgow than in Leeds or Manchester, but unwillingness to say "Please" or "Thank You" is widespread, and even female children are taciturn. There is no more hooliganism or destructiveness than in any other town with a large slum population, but there is a great lack of that spontaneous courtesy that is to be found among say the children of Stepney where the general level of character and probity is much lower than it is in Glasgow. Even among little girls, the standards of approach and refinements of life are rather heavily suppressed by the prevailing atmosphere.

When Glasgow girls come to the marriageable age, which is early in an industrial city, femininity comes into its own for a period that is as brief as the reign of the daffodil. A good many of the young girls are pretty, and a good many more are handsome, but the sensitive native feels that they lack something in suavity and the care for the graces which Lord Chesterfield so much cherished and admired. Brought up in grim and barely civilized conditions, the lower grades of proletarian females are hardly more capable of running a well-ordered house than they are of conducting an orchestra. These, of course, are a minority, and what is true of the minority in Glasgow is equally true of the minority in Warrington or Newcastle, but the legend of the frugal and conscientious Scottish wife requires considerable modification in view of industrial corruption. Some of the best women in the world live in Gorbals and Cowcaddens, but so do some women, young and old, who would be considered as letting the side down in an African kraal.

Apart from the submerged tenth (which surfaced spectacularly during the War), Glasgow women of the working class make an astonishingly good job of slum or near slum conditions which are calculated to destroy every civilized instinct in people of weak character. They are perhaps not quite so remarkable for making the most of the infinitely better conditions in the new housing estates. That is not through lack of will but through lack of knowledge. As in so many other industrial areas, the standard of housecraft among working-class women in Glasgow is not high.

Fifty years ago, Scottish housewives took an almost masochistic pride in cluttering their houses, particularly their kitchens, with objects which dirtied easily and rapidly and were exceedingly difficult to clean. The care of these objects was less a part of the domestic arts than a form of domestic athletics, having no practical use and giving no satisfaction except the satisfaction of doing something that was equally pointless and strenuous. The walls of small kitchens were lined with brass dish covers of different sizes, hung up on nails. These covers had been made to place over serving plates, but they were never used for any purpose at all. They simply hung shining on the wall and demanded a great deal of laborious cleaning. In every kitchen there was a grim black kitchen range with edges of shining steel, and the good housewife was judged by the condition of her range. The woman who was "house proud" was the faithful servant and attendant of her range. In fact, many a husband complained that the range received more loving care than himself or the children.

There was much that was admirable in this bustling devotion to a cause that may have been materialistic but was certainly not utilitarian, yet house pride is like any other kind of pride in that it is seldom sensible or proportioned. The scrubbing and scouring wives overdid the scrubbing and scouring, and many of them secretly regretted the loss of the range when they were transferred to more modern and brighter premises.

But the care and thought that were spent on these unnecessary exercises might have been more profitably spent in following pursuits with a better functional justification, for example, cooking. Many Glasgow housewives bake very well, but few of them know or care much about cooking. The fault does not lie with lack of skill but with conservatism, lack of enterprise and a deep suspicion of all materials that have not been made respectable by generations of local acceptance. Broths, fries, stews, sausages and a very limited (and expensive) range of fish set the bounds. Anything outside is classed as "nonsense" and probably dangerous nonsense. This extreme narrowness of choice is reflected in all but the most expensive Glasgow restaurants, for even in the days when food was plentiful, the whole menu could have been written on the back of a postcard. Bacon and egg, sausage and chips, sausage and egg and perhaps a piece of fried meat fairly well exhausted what the average restaurant supplied, because that was all the customers could be persuaded to choose from. The habits of home eating dominated choice in eating out. Either the women created and sustained the prejudice or else they submitted to the prejudice of the "men". During the War a voluntary canteen at the docks provided excellent egg dishes made from real, powdered eggs. For a while these were very popular and then one day the demand ceased almost totally. One of the men had inspected the waste bins and seen that there were no egg shells. That was the end of that.

In other respects, Glasgow women show a submissive conservatism that is not good for social advancement or a brighter life. Although the basic accent and intonation are much the same for most of the range of Glasgow society, the pronunciation of a large part of the working class is painfully slovenly. More than in most other places, clever children from working-class homes develop two forms of speech when they go to secondary schools, and, more than in most places, their more correct and civilized pronunciation is resented, rebuked and positively discouraged at home. The same attitude is displayed to the better manners and habits inculcated at school. It is hardly to be doubted that there would be more encouragement for the children if the mothers had the decisive voice, but in such things, as in most others, the arbiter is the "man".

Another adverse factor is the pressure of neighbours. For many generations, the women of Glasgow kept house in buildings that were appallingly overcrowded and where effective privacy was an impossibility. In such conditions, it was a rule of self-preservation to get on with the neigh-

"HING OOT"

bours, and the surest way not to get on with the neighbours was to set up to be "superior" or different in any way. Doors were left open or keys were left with the woman next door. The readiest and most pleasant form of converse for two women was the "hing oot". That is to say, a woman planted her elbows on the sill of her kitchen window and talked with the women "hinging oot" of the next kitchen window, a matter of a few feet away. Living on top of each other and nearly shoulder to shoulder, it took a rare and risky degree of moral courage to reject the accepted conventions. In his novel *Main Street*, Sinclair has given a picture of the social pressure that can be exercised in a close and narrow community, but his defiant heroine was so lucky she didn't know she was alive. Whatever inconveniences she suffered in Main Street, Gopher Prairie, if she had tried the same gesture of defiance in Main Street, Gorbals or Bridgeton, she would have been more heavily inconvenienced. Come to think of it, she might not have been alive.

Old habits die hard, even when they are inherited. The daughter of the woman who missed her kitchen range herself finds life in a Council Estate (or Scheme) lacking in the comfort of the old established patterns of close and continuous human contacts with the neighbours. The Schemes are airy, but they are also socially bleak, and women have been known to go back to the slums because they could not adjust themselves to a more reserved and private way of life. These, it must be insisted, are a tiny minority of the slackest and least intelligent, and their return was often connected with a strong aversion to paying more in rent than immemorial custom had sanctified. But even that aversion is an indication of ingrained and unthinking conservatism.

Against these social recidivists there must be set the women who have always desperately, but secretly, longed to "keep themselves to themselves". For them the greatest blessing of a Council house is the fact that the neighbours cannot breeze across the landing to borrow a bit of a loaf, or take a cup of tea and spend endless and empty hours in gossiping. Perhaps an even greater advantage of relative isolation is the partial opportunity it affords to keep the children away from the undisciplined, destructive and frequently foul-mouthed brats who inevitably set the tone in a slum area and whose barbaric behaviour is unchecked by public opinion because their equally undisciplined (and foul-mouthed) mothers would make life a screaming misery for any stuck-up piece who looked sideways at their weans.

This avoidance of trouble is another old habit that dies hard, and it explains the rather shocking destruction that goes on in Slum Clearance Schemes. If the women who have better habits and better ambitions had more self-confidence, they could do more to suppress the young hooligans than an army of police.

It is unsafe to generalize or even to draw hard and fast distinctions in such matters. The foulest-mouthed slum mother of my acquaintance cared for her children in a manner that was literally heroic. The words that came trippingly off her tongue would have shaken a policeman, but the teachers and the school nurse regarded her children as the cleanest, the best cared-for and also the best behaved in the school. Considering that she brought them up in a house that would hardly pass inspection for a stable, it took a highly exceptional character and devotion to do what she did.

Yet, it may be doubted if she would have made the best use of a modern house, or could have understood any higher ambitions than her own, if her children had felt them. She made, on the whole, a masterly job of life as she knew it, but she was helpless to lead any other kind of life. She was typical of her kind. She was a prisoner of her environment and her heredity, and the unquestioning follower of her "man". So far as the Glasgow working class are concerned, Ibsen wrote *A Doll's House* in vain.

CHAPTER SIX

WORK

TO any devout Marxist it goes without saying that the character of the Glasgow man and his social habits are a reflection of his economic conditions, but a good case could be made for the assertion that the Glasgow man has been formed more by religious than by industrial or commercial interests.

Glasgow achieved its first importance as a cathedral city. Hence the motto, "Let Glasgow Flourish by the Preaching of the Word." This motto had a practical as well as a pious meaning, for the medieval cathedral clergy drew substantial incomes from parishes outside the city, which must have been a satisfactory state of affairs for the honest burgesses who supplied them with the goods of this world. It was in the Cathedral that the University was born. This gave Glasgow further prestige and more economic advantages, but until the eighteenth century Glasgow remained a fairly small town, which straggled down the hill from the Cathedral and then stretched along the bank of the shallow Clyde. The University was not lacking in distinction, but the glory of the Cathedral had been much diminished by the Reformation, and although religious activity was strong, the Word was preached with a pugnacity which was anything but helpful to the material flourishing of Glasgow. Glasgow was considered by some visitors to be a singularly pleasant and even beautiful town, important for the West of Scotland and for Scotland at large, but not for the wide world.

After the Union of Parliaments, Glasgow commercial men began to move. They had always resented their exclusion from the "English" colonies, and the collapse of the Darien Scheme left them with bitter memories and a staggering deficit. But they seized on their new opportunities with both hands. They rapidly built up an impressive colonial trade. They were big men in the sugar world and, for a time, they were the biggest of all in tobacco.

This was the age of the Tobacco Lords, purse-proud and arrogant men who strutted the pavement at Glasgow Cross and expected that humbler citizens would keep their distance. Just before the outbreak of the American Revolution they had collared rather more than half of the American tobacco trade, but the Revolution finished them. Why this should be so is not entirely clear. After all, the Revolution was as inconvenient to Bristol as to Glasgow, but Bristol survived the blow and recovered its supremacy. There is reason to believe that the Glasgow men had over-reached themselves in their anxiety to capture trade and had invested too much in plantations and advanced too-extended credits. The Revolution brought bankruptcy to some of the most notable and unpopular men in the city. That particular age of swagger came to a sudden end.

But Glasgow continued to flourish through other men and by other means. The general merchants began to spread themselves ambitiously in international dealings, and the West of Scotland was for a time the leading place of cotton manufacture. Rothesay had the largest cotton mill in the world, and Robert Owen created in New Lanark an unbridled benevolent despotism. David

Dale, his even more eccentric father-in-law, scattered cotton mills as freely as he scattered religious counsel. (He taught himself Greek in middle-age so that he could study the Bible more closely and then opened his own church to expound his views.) The East End of Glasgow still bears dreary witness to the cotton age, but the chief mills were in Ayrshire and Stirlingshire. Still, they were the product of the city, for they were owned and controlled by Glasgow men, mostly general merchants who thought they would make cloth as well as sell it.

These men were considerably more inventive and enlightened than the tobacco lords, and were not at all contented with the narrow domestic life of stuffy comfort that had suited their fathers. Their handsome offices and mansion houses were the framework of central Glasgow as we know it to-day, and, as their ambition soared, they began to build those curious "Scottish baronial" castles which quaintly disfigure the Firth of Clyde.

Most of these were built, of course, in the nineteenth century, when cotton supremacy had already passed to Lancashire. Why it should have passed is a mystery no easier to explain than the decline of the tobacco trade. Admittedly, the introduction of steam-driven machinery destroyed the early advantage that the Scottish cotton industry enjoyed from the water-power supplied by the numerous and free-running rivers, but a well-founded industry should be able to survive the disappearance of the favourable handicap that gave it a flying start. After all, the great water wheel at Catrine kept running for generations after it had ceased to be the main source of power, and it is claimed that the new Catrine mill is the most modern in the world. It is hard to avoid the suspicion that the Glasgow men yielded the race to Manchester because they were more interested in something else. They were more commercially than industrially minded and not much inclined to devote their principal energies to maintaining one position against growing difficulties when more attractive opportunities were opening up in other directions.

There were the opportunities of the emerging heavy industries, and Glasgow made the most of these. If Lanarkshire coal and ore gave the ironmasters their start as water power gave the start to the cotton men, their greatest assets were inventiveness and enterprise. The deepening of the Clyde was a considerable and chancy feat, and Glasgow men led the world in the development of naval architecture for steam-driven vessels. Indeed, it might be said that Glasgow's contribution to the whole Steam-and-Iron Revolution would be hard to equal anywhere.

If commerce first made Glasgow prosperous, industry made her populous. The peace of the pleasant eighteenth-century city was destroyed, the teeming wynds where the immigrants gathered were the beginnings of the Glasgow slums which have become so well advertised by writers who have not always been moved by pure human compassion.

It is a curious illustration of a great change in social attitude that the moral indignation aroused by the slums a century ago was directed much less against the slums themselves than against the slum-dwellers. It was said with truth that the inhabitants of the wynds were dirty, drunken, shiftless, turbulent, and many of them idle and sexually loose. Reformers, and there were many of them, were more concerned with improving the slum dwellers than with improving the dwellings. Some had a touching faith in a miraculous change to be wrought by the teaching of literacy, while others put their reforming shirt on temperance or thrift. It was the great age of the insurance virtues, and few realized how appallingly difficult it was to practise these virtues in degrading conditions of dirt and overcrowding. If the Gorbals Story had been told a hundred years ago, the emphasis would have been laid on the moral responsibility and moral failure of the melodramatic gangsters and sluts.

There was undoubtedly a tinge of self-righteousness and a great lack of sympathetic imagination about the Victorian attitude to bad housing and its bad effects, but it was preferable to the economic determinism of to-day which asserts or implies that nobody can be blamed for anything, not even for the most atrocious deeds, if it can be shown that he was bred in bad physical surroundings. The Victorians at least paid men the compliment of believing that they could rise above their environment, and if there was too little sympathy for those who failed to make the effort, there was a great deal of selfless help and encouragement offered to those who did.

It is pointless to sneer at the Victorian middle class or to doubt the honesty of their purpose. Glasgow was growing at a furious rate and growing into a kind of city hitherto unknown on the earth. Existing laws and customs and habits of mind were not adjusted to the new conditions. The immense growth of the city and the dazzling achievements of the new inventions and techniques gave a heady sense of economic and social victory, with a corresponding lack of appreciation of the extent

of the casualty list. It was thought to be an age of opportunity for all and it was also thought that there was something wrong with those who failed to make opportunity
for themselves or take it when it was offered. It was a

"THE JAWBOX"

self-satisfied judgment and it was sometimes, but by no
means always, unjust.

It may seem dreadful to us that ignorant immigrants
should have been left to scramble out of the slums by
themselves or to sink into the mire, but at least they could

scramble out. If a man practised industry and other more difficult virtues he could establish himself in decency and comfort. But, to-day, there are people in Glasgow slums who have lived up to the highest standards of Samuel Smiles and yet have given up hope of ever escaping from their sordid surroundings. This is the fine fruit of a sensitive social conscience, but it would have struck the Victorians as being very immoral indeed.

Until the end of the nineteenth century there appears to have been no considerable revolt against the slums by the slum dwellers themselves. This is not so surprising as it sounds to modern ears. A great mass of highly selective and highly-coloured propaganda, often taught under the guise of history in schools, has spread the idea that poverty and squalor came into being with industrial capitalism, but, in fact, a large number of the original inhabitants of these slums rightly considered them to be a great improvement on the living conditions they had known before. The immigrants from Irish cabins or Hebridean black houses were often rebuked for their failure to make good and competent use of their much superior city housing. During the eighteenth century, a Glasgow timber merchant went down the river, on business, to Kilmun. After spending one night in a cottage of the picturesque Highland clachan, he asked, and received, permission to sleep for the rest of his time in the funeral vault of the Argyles. People who came from such romantic shielings would have been surprised to hear that they were victims because they were condemned to live in a house with stone walls, glass windows and a chimney which actually took the smoke away, regardless of how the wind was blowing.

Failure to understand and control the slum problem in time was deplorable but it was almost inevitable. The thriving spirit of the age was all for self-help, and it was much more concerned with expansion than with remedial care. But it must not be imagined that all the Glasgow working class lived in slums, at any time. The new race of skilled artisans lived in grim and bleak tenement blocks, but they lived there from choice. They had small sympathy with the English working-man's ambition to have his own front door and his own tiny patch of grass or garden. They wanted a dwelling that was solid and warm and roomy, and that demand could only be supplied by the tenement system. They regarded the artisan cottage as a tiny and gimcrack affair, not at all fitted for a serious-minded Clydesider who knew good and lasting stonework when he saw it.

Unfortunately, some of the work put into Glasgow housing was a good deal too solid. When shifts of population brought the slum tide overlapping into once "respectable" working-class districts, the houses had centuries of life before them. They became bug-infested and decrepit inside, but they stood four-square and strong enough to blunt the teeth of Time itself. There are slum houses in the legendary Gorbals that are enormously superior in structure to almost any house in a prosperous English suburb.

Yet, it would be idle to deny that the problem of slums in Glasgow, or rather, in the industrial West, owed something, even a good deal, to man's inhumanity to man. Some of the masters of the Iron Age were as tough as the material they handled. They had none of the culture to which some of the earlier merchants could pretend, and they had thought for nothing except industrial expansion, particularly the expansion of their own firm. To them it may be that slums were like slagheaps, unsightly enough but necessary, and they were far from delicate either in æsthetic or moral feeling. Their descendants have lost much of the ruthless and grasping qualities of the family founders, and are not entirely assured that a large steel works is its own absolute justification and the noblest work of God, though it may well be that in losing some of the intimidating self-regard and self-confidence of their fathers they have lost some quality of drive and daring as well.

The most truly representative Glasgow man is not the employer, old style or new, but the industrial artisan who has changed very little with the years. His standard of skill is very high indeed, and his work is plain, solid and unpretentious, like the food he prefers to eat and the kind of house he prefers to live in. There are no frills and no nonsense about Glasgow craftsmanship, and the men who work in the shipyards need hardihood as well as skill. Working on a ship on a wet and bitter winter's day is nobody's idea of a joke, and there is also a good deal of danger. The man who stands on a high scaffolding and picks up red-hot rivets casually thrown to him is not easily perturbed by the minor trials of a manual worker's life. But the riveter is not among the aristocracy of shipyard workers. The most important of these men are the so-called "engineers", the fitters and turners whose industrial skill and training are unsurpassed anywhere in the world. Many of them have served for years on ships, with officer rank, and they have known men and cities. Their level of intelligence and experience is high indeed. A generation ago, it was a commonplace for such men, in their later years, to move into the middle class, taking a house in some unpretentious suburb or a flat in a tenement suburb nearer to their work, and end their days as manual operatives of the *bourgeoisie*. But for more than a generation these same men have voted solidly for a political Party and a political philosophy which have worked for their undoing. There was a time within the memory of the middle-aged when the skilled man earned twice as much as the unskilled. To-day, the "differential" is hardly worth counting, and certainly not worth serving an apprenticeship for.

The slow declension of their relative advantage in wages and prestige has had much less effect on them than their shattering experience of unemployment between the Wars. In those dismal years skilled men counted themselves lucky to get jobs as tram conductors or picture-house attendants, and those who were not lucky emigrated by the tens of thousand to the United States and Canada. Being more alive to the meaning and movement of economic forces than a highly provincial community like the miners, they were less given to self-pity and their plight was less thoroughly advertised, but the bleak and hopeless years had a strong effect upon them. All the melancholy aspects of the Deserted Village were reproduced in John Brown's and Fairfield's and further down the river. When work was stopped on the *Queen Mary* a blight descended on Clydebank and farther afield. Men felt and said that the Clyde was finished. The great cranes, like huge Meccano storks, stood over yards where grass was growing. Unemployment was miserable everywhere, but on Clydeside it was spectacular; it brought the hopeless and stricken silence of the plague.

War brought back full employment to the Clydeside, and full employment has persisted ever since. But the Glasgow artisan is still uneasy. The experience of idleness bit deep, and, of course, the thousands who emigrated have gone for ever. There is a constant fear that unemployment may return like a tornado, to lay the shipyards waste once again. It cannot be said that there is much disposition to study the causes of unemployment. It is regarded as a scourge inflicted unpredictably and irrationally on the worthy proletariat either by blind forces beyond all human control or else by a species of political Furies known as "The Tories". It should be noted that the word "Tory" is almost completely divorced from any connection with the Conservative Party. A prominent industrialist will always be spoken of as a Tory. If it is pointed out that he is in fact a pillar of strength to the Liberal Party, this correction will be dismissed as an idle and disingenuous frivolity.

The Tories are the exploiters, and exploiters are not popular. There is a happy tale, entirely untrue, which illustrates the combative nature of the Glasgow working man. It is said that during the War a Union branch determined to have a really high-class motto. One of their temporary members was a dilutee, with some claim to secondary education. They commissioned him to produce a motto in Latin. After some pondering he produced this suggestion: "Nil Carborundum illegitimi". The members asked him rather suspiciously what this meant. He explained that it meant, "Don't let the bastards grind you down." They were amply satisfied.

But there are some signs of a growing suspicion that the Tories are not the only people to inflict injustice on the artisan. Full employment has done nothing whatever to restore the relative advantage of the skilled man, but rather the reverse. This is beginning to rankle. Fairly soft jobs that demand no intelligence and no training are paid as well as the most arduous and difficult work in shipyards and engineering shops. The skilled men feel that they are losing more than their appropriate financial reward. They are also losing social recognition of their superior status and worth. The magic incantation of the solidarity of the proletariat has hitherto confined the expression of this feeling to private and guarded grumblings, but it may yet become a formidable disruptive influence in the "Socialist Movement" and certainly could be made formidable if the Tories knew any more about the Socialists than the Socialists know about them.

One of the worst evils of unemployment was the feeling it induced in men that they were unwanted, with their skill and energy despised. The flattening out of wage levels had induced a modified feeling of the same kind. The skilled man does not feel that he is not wanted, but he does feel that the worth of his skill is disregarded.

There is fortunately no diminution in the hearty spirit of independence. Any Clydeside employer who expected his men to treat him with deference or feudal loyalty would be indulging in strange fancies indeed. To do them justice, few if any of the employers expect or want anything more than man-to-man dealings, and that is certainly all they ever get. In the prosperous days before the first World War, the shipyard workers were expected to return to work on a certain Monday which marked the end of the Summer Fair holidays. They used to gather solemnly outside the shipyard gates and go through the ceremony of "tossing the brick". They threw a brick into the air. If it came down again, they stayed off for a day or two more. If it stayed up in the air, then they would go back to work. This was characteristic of their attitude then, and no less now.

There came the days when tossing the brick no longer seemed funny. These were days when men ate their hearts out for year after year. The relief work that could be provided for the unemployed was not such as these men could do for any length of time. Middle-aged fitters do not make good navvies. What other work could be sought out meant an abandonment of a life-long skill. The shipyard men who found alternative employment had stepped down in the industrial world. Their "trade" had no longer any use for them. They had been struck off the industrial register. They took it quietly, either unemployment or the retreat to some inferior work, but they felt it deeply. Yet, when the great demand came for all trained men to go back in the yards, many of those who had found other jobs were unwilling to give them up. They had eaten the meagre bread of idleness once before and they did not want to run the risk of having to eat it again. The men still have a pride in their work, but they have not yet recovered an assured faith that their work will always be wanted.

Shipbuilding and heavy engineering are, of course, not the only major occupations in Glasgow. Indeed, most of the famous yards are beyond the City boundaries, in Greenock, Port Glasgow, Clydebank and Dunbarton. Glasgow docks are of considerable importance and they have given less trouble since the War than the docks of Liverpool and London, largely because the dockers have their own union which is excellently run. There are many factories, large and small. Templeton's, the carpet firm, have a world-wide high-quality trade. They have provided carpets for the White House and for Westminster Abbey. Their main factory, standing on Glasgow Green, is an exact replica of a Venetian Palace. It looks extremely odd.

There are firms of international reputation for the making of precision instruments. I once rather profitlessly read a novel in French about the Japanese Navy. It was rather less than thrilling, until I came across a reference to a "telemetre Barr et Stroud", and I felt at once that I was back home again. Whisky is of course a Glasgow product of well-merited fame. There are large chemical works. "Tennant's Stalk" which once dominated the northern skyline has now been demolished, but it was for long an object of faintly derisive affection and pride. The bagpipe industry cannot be regarded as one of the major elements in the world's economy, but it is something that Glasgow should provide bagpipes for Afghanistan as well as for the more conventional home market.

There are roughly fifteen thousand factories in Glasgow, producing the endless and fantastic variety of objects without which the industrialized world feels unable to survive.

But what is truly surprising is the work that is not there. In the years when Glasgow was wallowing in a miserable trough of depression, the South of England was developing a great many new industries and prospering exceedingly. It is understandable that Glasgow should be handicapped in the production of light articles where freight charges loom largely in the selling cost and where it is a huge advantage for the maker to be near the chief markets. But it is less easy to find a reason why Glasgow should have done so little in the way of producing motor cars and aircraft. With the wealth of manual and designing skill available, Glasgow might well have become the British Detroit, but that did not happen.

As has been noted earlier, the reputation of Red Clydeside discouraged the heads of the newer industries from seeking opportunities there. The high traditions of "militancy", of "solidarity" of "political consciousness" might sound very well in the columns of *Forward* or the *Daily Worker*, but these words made no sweet music in the ears of employers who preferred to seek more docile labour in places where there was no noble tradition at all.

Glasgow's unfortunate reputation for strikes was achieved over a very brief period, beginning in the "Labour Withholding Committee" during the first World War, and lasting till the Forty Hours strike a few years after the end of the War. Many of the strikes of this time were undoubtedly political and some of them were even revolutionary in a half-hearted and unimpressive way. But this fiery and Russian-inspired mood was snuffed out in one afternoon's rioting which the police dealt with very efficiently, and since then Glasgow's record of strikes is no worse than the average and perhaps better. But that short-lived effort was given immense newspaper publicity and the reputation has stuck like tar to this day. Undoubtedly it has done damage, though how much it would be quite impossible to say.

But whatever weight may be attached to this explanation, it implies that industrial initiative and development in the West of Scotland must be sponsored and capitalized from England and even further afield. Scottish capitalists could hardly be deterred by vague memories of sensational headlines in newspapers read fifteen years before. They knew their own men better than that.

What then did deter the Glasgow capitalists from striking out on their own and making use of the immense advantages they had at their hand? Why were there no Scottish Nuffields or Austins or De Havillands? It is hard to think of a complimentary answer. Certainly earlier generations would not have been content to sit back and watch others conquering all the new worlds. The men who drained the Clyde, the men from Fairfields, and the other yards who made revolutionary history in marine engineering would have leapt at the glowing opportunities offered by the internal combustion engine. They would have been first in the field and not have waited till somebody else asked them if they would not like to take a hand in the game.

In the days of Glasgow's rapid expansion, the men who made the city expand were exceedingly ready to take a chance and also ready to switch from one thing to another quite different. The qualities they showed are not those generally regarded as being characteristically Scottish, but they paid handsome dividends (with occasional bankruptcies). It is difficult to escape the suspicion that their grandsons and great-grandsons had grown stuffy and conservative. That blight of unenterprise that afflicted all British industry lay thick and heavy on Glasgow. Glasgow industrialists followed the old ways with dogged persistence and it is not even certain that even in the old ways they were noticeably better than their upstart competitors. For example, it would be hard to persuade a Newcastle man that the Clyde had anything to teach the Tyne in the way of ship design, or, indeed, in any other way.

In fact the aircraft and motor industry which does now exist is the result of War emergency or of English investment. Those who worked most earnestly for years to vary Glasgow's industry were chiefly concerned with tempting English firms to open branches, and much of the post-War development is a result of Government support, not perhaps always wisely given. To a considerable extent, the West of Scotland has been colonized.

The workers of the bitter memories who denounce the exploitation of the capitalists would be better employed if they denounced the failure of the local capitalists to exploit. There was something far wrong when the most ambitious and most successful industrial scheme for years was a device for buying up shipyards and selling them for tennis courts or for any other purpose, on the strict condition that they must not be used again to build ships. If the same workers cared to indulge in a little self-examination, which is not a habit of workers, they might reflect that the honest pride they felt in their militant reputation thirty years ago was possibly misplaced, and that the brutal capitalists could hardly be blamed if they were shy of investing sums for the sake of giving the workers extended opportunities of demonstrating their solidarity.

Glasgow's heavy industry is so well-known that there is a tendency to forget that Glasgow is also an important commercial city. As a supply centre for consumer goods, it is not merely the greatest in Scotland, but no other town comes anywhere near it. There is not the immense

6

mass of clerks and typists to be found in London, but their numbers are considerable. Not only does Glasgow supply an overwhelming proportion of the Scottish domestic demand, but there are firms with enormous overseas dealings. Close connections with India and Burma have long provided comfortable jobs for Glasgow agents, estate managers, civil engineers and chartered accountants who would otherwise have been rather poorly paid at home. These men are the "exiles" who sit down and weep when they remember Zion. All over the world they form Scottish clubs of one kind or another and celebrate Burns's Nicht and Saint Andrew's Day with bagpipes and blatherskite. A high proportion show no particular ambition to go home, but when the wine flows freely in Canada or Karachi their eyes mist over with regretful tears and they can even bring themselves to be polite to the Edinburgh man across the table. They are Glasgow's expendable surplus of trained men. The fact that they find it so easy to secure foreign posts says a good deal for their training and their character.

The biggest employer in Glasgow is the Corporation. There are round about forty thousand men and women on the municipal pay roll working in a great variety of services from psychiatry to dust collecting. It appears to be easier for a Corporation employee than for others to get a "Scheme" house, and some of them are able to live almost entirely outside the profit-making economy. Their Scheme house is publicly owned, they do most of their shopping in the Co-op, they travel by municipal transport and send their children to municipal schools. Likely enough they lodge their money in a trustee Savings Bank. They are the Municipal Men. They explain why a suburb like Knightswood which is almost painfully middle class has such a strong Socialist vote.

The Municipal Men have a better use for a local vote than most people. It is on the vote that their level of earnings depends and the rent of their subsidized houses, not to mention the amenities and advantage of their housing Scheme. As the Socialists have a more carefree attitude towards public expenditure than the reactionaries of the other side, they can command the allegiance of thousands who, by their income level and their habits of life, might be expected to vote against them.

There is a certain amount of resentment against the favoured and secure position of the municipal worker, whether professional, artisan or unskilled. This resentment was acutely felt during the depression years when workers in the private field not only lived in terror of the sack from week to week, but also had very poor wages when work was to be had. By contrast, the Corporation workers were well paid and they enjoyed that security which has become the passionate desire of the British proletariat. Even now, when security is, for the moment, enjoyed by all, the resentment persists. The Municipal Man enjoys contractual security, at the expense of the workers who are exposed to economic storms. So long as Glasgow lasts and votes are valued, his employment is secure. But the worker outside of the charmed and privileged circle still lives in dread of the day when mysterious forces which he does not even try to understand will deprive him once again of his livelihood. The Glasgow worker is much more intelligent and levelheaded than most, but his fear of unemployment is emotional and instinctive. It is the fear of a man who has been badly injured in a car smash and cannot take a rational view of the normal risks of the road. He is the fox who never had a tail, and he is irritated by the ample, bushy rear ornament of the protected Corporation class.

Needless to say, the most unpopular of the Corporation employees are the police. The majority of the proletariat regard them with a sincere, spontaneous and unqualified dislike. There is nothing that the police can do about it, for they are disliked not so much for what they are as for what they stand for. They conduct raids on street bookies and enforce a positively Rabbinical observance of the closing hours for pubs. They are regarded as the servants not merely of the capitalists, but also of the Puritan. They are large, well-fed men. Many of them are Highland. In a town where the ruling classes, whether economic, social or religious, impose standards which the common people neither accept nor effectively defy, the police could hardly fail to be unpopular. The Glasgow police have certainly succeeded. They are mostly decent men, and they do not seem to be worried about it.

Next to the police in unpopularity are the transport workers. The drivers and conductors of trams and buses have no very cordial relations with their passengers. They serve them better than the London transport workers do, but with less surface geniality and with a good deal more friction. One Glasgow artisan was charged with trying to swindle the Transport Department out of a penny fare. He took the case right to the House of Lords, and won. Glasgow was with him to a man.

Teachers enjoy a modified unpopularity. The local respect for education is in their favour, but against them is the fact that they are believed to live on the rates and to do very little work for their salaries. The length of their holidays is a topic for brooding and censorious envy on the part of those who have ten days at the Fair, and there is a deeper sense of grievance not so clearly realized. What they teach in school in the way of speech and manners and customs is an implicit criticism of the example given by a large proportion of parents at home, particularly in the slums. In a startlingly large number of Glasgow homes, the vocabulary of the parents might most kindly be described as Anglo-Saxon, and there is an aggressive attitude of "No nonsense", with the implication that some of the most primitive elements of civilized living are unworthy and debasing frivolities. The teachers oppose this attitude because they must, but there are not a few parents who resent an education which teaches their children to be critical of themselves. They doubly resent having to pay rates to support the educators. They are trebly resentful when they do not pay their rates.

But neither the municipal employees nor the workers in the supply services and in general commerce set the tone of Glasgow. That is set by the workers in heavy industry. There is not a millionaire in Glasgow nor a University Professor who would not feel lessened in his own esteem if he became the subject of the derisive hostility of riveters or boiler-scalers. The men with the hard and dirty hands may resent their imagined social inferiority, but they dominate the thought and feeling of Glasgow more than they know. The city was made by the men of the manual arts and crafts, and the city remembers that fact, which is ever evident. All of Glasgow lives on top of its primary source of wealth and well-

being. There is no escaping from the hard facts of industrial life, and it is as well.

The industrial workers are emotional and they suffer
strikingly from a transferred Calvinism, which gives an
odd logic and intensity to notions which are unrealistic
and sometimes exceedingly peculiar. But their qualities
of character are valuable indeed. They can beat the
English flat out for their laconic and undemonstrative
acceptance of things as they are.

During the late War two Glasgow soldiers met in a
pub and struck up a drinking acquaintance. Both were
the horny-handed type, with no pretensions to be other
than they were. In the course of talk, it emerged that
both had been at Dunkirk. "When did you get away?"
said one to the other. "Thursday," was the answer.
"Gosh, you were lucky," said the first with fervent simplicity. "It rained like hell on the Friday."

That was the Glasgow worker. It was a long tradition
of hard training that gave this man his balanced and temperate view of life, weighing the lesser evil against the
greater and finding the lesser harder to bear.

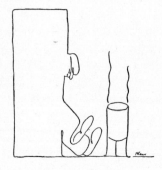

CHAPTER SEVEN

PRAYER

GLASGOW is a religious city. The statement can be made with some confidence, but it might give rise to serious misunderstanding, if it was not considerably extended and qualified. Glasgow is not one of those religious cities where people go to church. Nor is it even one of those cities where people give a full interior assent to the national faith, but do not find it convenient to practise their faith. But Glasgow is religious in the sense that religion is taken seriously even by the atheists. It is still a live issue. The amiable indifference of the English masses is not to be found in Glasgow. The Kirk has been too prominent and aggressive in the past, and the people have been too well pounded with theology over the centuries for the Kirk to sink into the position of being a barely noticeable, faintly unpopular and slightly picturesque part of the background of life.

The taste for theological discussion is no longer widespread, though the habit of mind remains. Only thirty years ago, I stood on Fair Saturday night on Rothesay Pier and listened to an argument. A group of artisans were discussing the personal existence of the devil. They talked soberly and to the point and with much repetition and careful explanation of the obvious, in the high Scottish manner. There were also on the pier a number of men so far gone in liquor that it looked as if they would never return. The noises they made were neither religious nor refined. They were on high holiday and they were certainly high. But against this background of boisterous noise the disputants plodded earnestly on. A considerable crowd gathered, listening with genuine interest, some of them throwing in an occasional objection or suggestion. It was like a medieval disputation in a modest way, and it lasted for hours.

To-day I fear that any such argument would centre on Stalin as the Prince of Darkness, or else would turn on the question as to whether religion was, or was not, the opiate of the people, but the earnestness, and also the repetition, would be the same. The so-called Presbyterians of Glasgow have opted out of the Kirk in massive numbers, but they have not forgotten about it, and the Kirk does not allow them to forget. The Kirk is still a part of their lives, even though for many it is a part they would rather do without.

There can be no question of the opting-out. An American came to live in Glasgow some years before the War. Having looked round, he announced, "This town is over-capitalized for churches." He was right. This excessive capitalization is partly explained by the great Disruption of 1843. The leaders of the Free Church, who had broken away from the Establishment, claimed to be the true and legitimate Church of Scotland. No Scottish Presbyterians meekly accept the position of Dissenters. The smallest Presbyterian sect claims to be the only legitimate inheritor of the Gospel truth and the discipline derived from John Knox and Geneva. If the vast majority reject that claim so much the worse for the vast majority.

Of all secessions that of the Free Church was by far the most formidable. The men who organized it had the will and means to beard the Erastian Establishment in every parish in the land, and they did so. Thus, many a small village found itself dowered with two churches, and perhaps three, Established, Free and United Presbyterian. The evidence of godly zeal was impressive indeed, but there was also a faint suspicion of a less spiritual quality, human combativeness and a determination to show that the men who had cut the trammels of State control, could do every bit as well as the unworthy clerics who relied on Pharaoh's horses and chariots and enforced contributions.

The great split had a very stimulating effect on the Established Church. The immense sums contributed voluntarily to the Free Kirk and smaller bodies provoked a spirit of emulation among the more easy-going members of the Establishment. They became more active and enormously more generous in their support for the Church, both at home and in the mission field. Competition had its customary invigorating effect.

Yet, the Free Kirk was always more energetic than the Established and it probably did more to alienate the industrial proletariat. The great split which created the Free Kirk came on narrow points of the relations of Church and State, and in the beginning the two rival churches had no other differences. But differences soon appeared on other grounds, though not on the theological. In the nineteenth century virtually every established minister voted Conservative in the University Parliamentary elections, where the votes were openly recorded. Virtually every Free Kirk minister voted Liberal.

This might appear to indicate that the Free Kirk was more in touch with the working class, but it was not so. The wealthy laymen in the Free Kirk were industrialists whose Liberal doctrine was firmly based on uncompromising *laisser-faire*. For them, Smiles's Self Help almost ranked among the apocrypha. Thrift, industrious striving and personal independence came very high in their catalogue of virtues. As a result, the Puritanism of the Free Kirk was doubly distilled. Teetotalism became a positive act of faith, and anti-gambling became something like an obsession. In Victorian times, this rigorous attitude commanded at least a theoretical assent from the artisans of the cities, but it was very far from popular in the crowded slums where life was startingly free from inhibitions of any kind, except an inhibition against saving. The slum-dwellers knew that large numbers of the *bourgeoisie* put on an expression of grief and pain when they passed a pub door, but they had a deep and well-founded suspicion that in many a comfortable home the grocery bills were heavily loaded on the liquid side. They believed that the rich wanted to impose austerity standards on the poor, which they did not at all intend to follow themselves.

The belief did injustice to many honest and earnest men, both clerical and lay, but there was enough truth in it to do great harm to the Presbyterian Kirks, particularly the Secession Kirks. There were men of a double conscience whose conduct brought some of the taint of hypocrisy to their social gospel of Puritan uplift. Even in the twentieth century it was possible for men to object to the Corporation golf clubs being open on Sundays, while they themselves broke the Sabbath on a seaside

course, away from neighbours' eyes. The same dis-
ingenuousness, to put it no more strongly, was shown
during the period of the Local Option voting.

Local Option was a curious device by which every city
ward and country district voted for or against Prohibition.
The results were curious. In the royal and ancient Burgh
of Rutherglen, just over the river from Glasgow, one side
of the Main Street was wet and the other dry. In Glasgow
itself, some of the suburban districts went dry, but it was
known that men who voted to keep their home ward dry
voted from their business addresses to keep their business
ward wet. They did not want the social degradation of a
public house near their homes, but they did very sincerely
want a drink, and so the people who lived in the centre
of the city had to put up with the degradation. Such conduct did nothing to commend the temperance cause.

It must be repeated that the charge of hypocrisy against
the Puritan body was, and is, grossly exaggerated, but
hypocrites there were—and are. For example, there was
that very eminent Victorian who ran the City of Glasgow
Bank. He was such a strict Sabbatarian that he refused
to read a Monday morning newspaper because it had
been printed on Sunday. Yet, when his Bank folded up
and honest men were ruined and the commercial life of
Glasgow came nearly to a standstill, it was discovered
that he had been swindling on a royal scale for many
years. During the period of his brigandage new directors
were elected to the Board from time to time. They should
not have failed to learn the true facts of the situation, but
none of them talked.

The case of Lord Overtoun was different. He was a
man of the strictest honesty, and he supported Free Kirk

causes on a truly magnificent scale. He was a deeply religious man who had prayer meetings in the great chemical works. But when Keir Hardie published the wages paid to unskilled labourers in the works the public reaction was violent and the Kirk suffered along with the capitalist.

It would be quite unfair to say that the Free Kirk was ever under the dominance of hard-fisted, narrow-minded capitalists. The men who left their secure livings to live entirely by voluntary offerings, were men breaking away from what they conceived as domination, and the great Chalmers, the author of the Disruption, was the most ardent social reformer of his time. If the Free Kirk was stern and absolute in its demands, the rigorous spirit was the fruit of real conviction.

Still, there was some plausibility in the ingenious argument advanced by some apologists for the Establishment. They claimed that the Established Kirk was more truly independent than the Free. The Established minister was not under even an unconscious pressure to shape his message with one eye on the collection plate. He could stand up to the wealthiest of his parishioners with no thought of the debt on the organ. He could also stand up to the whole congregation which was more important. At all levels of income the Free Kirk members were ready givers, and it was more difficult for the minister to quarrel with the whole body of his flock than with one rich member. The Presbyterian system is highly democratic and the minister is in no position to issue ultimatums to his congregation. He must try to bring them along with him, but it may happen that the congregation brings him along with them. It is a fair surmise that in any congregation the most generous subscribers are the most active members, on the whole. The active membership of the Free Kirk was overwhelmingly Puritan and set the tone of the Kirk, most emphatically in its social attitude.

By English standards the Established Kirk looked very far from tolerant, but nevertheless it was more tolerant than the Secession Kirks. Full respect was paid to the Sabbath, but teetotalism was not an absolute article of faith. It was possible for members to join the Temperance Movement of the Established Kirk by simply pledging themselves to be temperate. There was no inclination to follow the example of some Free Churches where even the sacramental wine was non-alcoholic, and men who were otherwise the strictest fundamentalists insisted that the wine of the Scriptures was not wine at all but unfermented juice. Worse still, there were Established churches where the abomination of bazaar raffles was tolerated. Because of this highly relative mildness, there were Established Ministers who were regarded with good-humoured affection by non-church-goers. Norman McLeod, for example, became a part of popular mythology. The stories told about him were not flattering to the cloth and they were also totally untrue, but they were proof of a human and endearing personality. He was not condemned as one of the "unco guid", that deadly accusation. There were many Free Kirk ministers who were regarded with affectionate respect by their own congregations, but few indeed who became the object of good-natured gossip and public interest beyond the confines of their own communion.

The Free Kirk also incurred unpopularity among the educated classes by the heresy hunts which were followed in Victorian Scotland as closely as a good murder trial. The "Intellectuals" were scandalized by the determined attack on men of real eminence like Robertson Smith by combative conservatives like "Faithful" Begg. The scandal of the clerks was hardly fair. The fundamentalists may have been hopelessly out-classed in argument, but nothing could alter the fact that they were defending the historic position of their Church, while the heretics were undermining that position. Whatever elements of absurdity there might be in the heresy hunts, no one denied the right of a man like Robertson Smith to accept the conclusions to which his researches had led him. What the conservative element did question was the compatibility of these conclusions with the Free Kirk ministry. They won a temporary success but they were fighting against the tide. Calvinism, Biblical literalism and Presbyterian discipline were increasingly questioned within the Kirks and almost totally rejected outside.

A somewhat unexpected complaint against some of the Secession Kirks, was the charge of snobbery. It happened on more than one occasion that a church was founded in an unfashionable district by a few faithful and earnest men. As the years went on, the church flourished, the faithful men prospered, but the district declined. The faithful departed to more agreeable quarters and built a new and more handsome church, leaving the old one behind as a kind of mission hall. The poor regarded such transferences without enthusiasm. Their feelings were expressed by the rhyme chalked by a workman on an expensive new church in Great Western Road.

"This church wasn't built for the poor and needy,
  But for the rich and Doctor Eadie".

Dr. Eadie was a well-known and fashionable minister.

At the turn of the century, the Free Kirk joined with the United Presbyterians to form the United Free Kirk and a quarter of a century later the United Free rejoined the Establishment. It goes without saying that each union was marked by a new secession, but after the second union more than nine-tenths of the Scottish Presbyterians were enrolled in one national church. The terms reached with the State were highly advantageous. The united Church of Scotland enjoys the prestige and the material benefits of establishment, while it also enjoys total freedom from State interference. The position reached might well be the envy of Anglicans, but it was reached too late.

In many respects the condition of the Church of Scotland is impressively healthy. The clergy have a high general level of literary education, though the depths of their theology may leave some room for doubt. For the most part they are men of public spirit who lead honourably useful lives. Among them there are men of great learning and commanding intellect. The extent of the missionary effort is astonishing for such a small nation, and the influence of Scottish Presbyterianism is strongly felt in the Dominions and even in the United States. The General Assembly busies itself with the affairs of the nation, both spiritual and material, and among educated men it commands an amount of attention which Convocation could never hope to reach in England. The Church of Scotland as by law established is still a very powerful force in the land, but it suffers from one simple and fatal weakness. The people no longer believe in it.

Of the working classes in Glasgow who are nominally Presbyterians only a handful ever go to church at all. Most of them are not merely indifferent. They are hostile, not to the doctrine of the Church which does not interest them at all, but to the discipline. Thought of the minister and the Kirk Session stirs in them an atavistic uneasiness, and they are well aware that their opportunities for human enjoyment are restricted by the clerical lobby in Town Councils and elsewhere which works successfully in defiance of majority opinion. They are not at all impressed by the fact that a notable number of the younger ministers have an active social conscience and even profess themselves Socialists. Their quarrel with the Kirk goes deeper than the battle of capitalist and proletarian. It is the quarrel that flared up into lawlessness of a mild kind with the "Sunday Breakers".

These were men who took Sunday excursions by steamer down the Clyde, away from a city that was far from beautiful and on Sunday was as dead as a cemetery. They found the turnstiles of the piers of the seaside resorts locked against them. They broke through and defeated this particular challenge of Sabbatarianism by physical force, but they did not forget. Yet, they have seldom won so complete a victory and workers have turned against the godly because they still deny them cakes and ale.

A sizeable proportion of the Glasgow middle class still attend church regularly or now and again. They have plenty of room. One prominent merchant of the last generation was rather proud of the fact that there were seldom more than a dozen in the church of which he was an elder. "We are not so much of a church," he explained, "as a kind of speeritual club." Others attend out of family tradition or convention or to win good marks for respectability.

There are also those who attend from motives of sincere

THE MEENISTER COMES TO TEA

religion, but is doubtful how far their religion could be called Presbyterian. The Scottish national Kirk is bound to the Westminster Confession of Faith, which is a document having none of the useful ambiguity of the Thirty-nine Articles. How many of the Kirk members accept the inescapable teachings of that document? It is safe to say that even among the regular and entirely conscientious church attenders only a fairly small minority could

7

put their hands on their hearts and declare that they believe it all.

Many of the clergy interpret the Confession in a Pickwickian sense. I once heard a prominent minister declare in public that he flatly rejected the idea of eternal punishment, but accepted the idea of temporal punishment. I suggested to him in private that he was denying the doctrine of Hell on which his church insisted and accepting the doctrine of Purgatory which his church denounced. He said, "Yes, but what else can I do?" Faithful Begg could have given him an answer, but the attitude was typical enough. If the people have turned against the discipline of Calvinism, the clergy show no disposition to expound or defend the fullness of the doctrine. There are no heresy hunts in the twentieth century and there are none of the doctrinal rows which occasionally make headlines for the Church of England, but the reason for the peaceful atmosphere in the theological field is not a united belief in traditional teachings but a tacit agreement to let these matters drop and to talk earnestly and at length about something else.

As Presbyterianism lost its public hold by its extreme Puritan emphasis, it lost its theological conviction by the penetration of German scholarship. The smaller Secession Kirks may still cling to the Confession of Faith, but they have little importance in Glasgow. Presbyterianism as an articulated and confident assertion of faith and as a code of discipline has lost Glasgow almost completely and, it seems, for ever.

Among the Protestant community the only serious rival to the Established Kirk is the Episcopal Church in Scotland. Its members are known as Episcopalians.

Earlier generations of more confident Presbyterians called them "Piskies" in a spirit of unkindly derision.

> Pisky, Pisky-Palian
> Doon on your hunkers and up again.

This rhyme once chanted by children indicates one of the handicaps under which the Episcopal Church suffers. Calvinism has bred into the Scottish mind a deep suspicion of religious ritual. The worship of God in the beauty of holiness is an austere ideal which wins the warm approval of people who themselves show no disposition to worship God in any circumstances whatever. The Episcopalians are thought to be half-way to Rome, which is very nearly the same as being half-way to the other place. They are also thought to be Anglicized. Socially, this charge had some contemporary validity, for many of the episcopal clergy are English, but it comes ill from a spiritual descendant of John Knox to complain of English intrusion into Scottish religious affairs.

The devastating distortions of school history books tell heavily against the Episcopal Church. The Episcopalians may claim to be the one, true national church with all the authority of historical continuity, but they are represented in text-books in a very ungainly light. They are alleged to be the supporters of an ecclesiastical system which royal tyranny and English cruelty tried unsuccessfully to foist upon the Scots.

It is not suggested that school children take the keenest interest in these (or any other) chapters of their history books, but the great curse of school history is that it creates prejudice and firm convictions which remain long after the supporting information, true or false, has been forgotten. It is difficult to shake a prejudice which has survived all the evidence that might make it faintly respectable. It is the unmerited handicap of the Episcopal Church in Scotland that it is regarded as being either socially or nationally an uncharacteristic and even a foreign body.

But it may well be that its greatest handicap for those who believe in its doctrine and its mission is the fact that it has an attraction for the snobbish. The Episcopal Church has a certain County flavour. It has the air of an unestablished Establishment, and the small and untypical Glasgow minority who have a good deal of money, social ambitions and a public school background tend to drift towards it. This must be discouraging for the underpaid and overworked clergy who faithfully serve a small and unrepresentative minority church, and at the same time are suspected of assumptions of superiority, of an old school cassock complex.

The position of the Episcopal Church in Scotland is very roughly like the position of the Church of Ireland. That is to say, it is a church which commands the allegiance of a large number of the gentry and the established families, but is suspect by the great majority as much for national as for religious reasons. The analogy is very imperfect, for the gulf between the Episcopal Church and the mass of the people is enormously greater in Ireland than in Scotland, and the national divergence is also enormously greater. It must also be conceded that the Scottish Episcopalians can hardly claim the remarkable intellectual record of their Irish brethren.

In fact, their church is of less importance in Glasgow

than it is in the country districts of Scotland. It is largely a church of the well-to-do, strengthened by a fair number of English residents, and slightly embarrassed by a certain amount of Orange support. The North of Ireland Protestants living in Glasgow and neighbourhood who happen to be practising Episcopalians are not much given to the cool quietism of Herbert and Vaughan. Many, though not all of them, find it difficult and quite unnecessary to separate the practice of their own religion from a pugnacious hostility to the Catholic Church. Anything which smacks of Romish practices rouses their stern opposition. In fact, one little Episcopal church near Glasgow was closed almost as soon as it was opened, because the predominantly North of Ireland congregation refused to tolerate the ritual employed and took a highly Presbyterian attitude towards their bishop when he exerted his authority. It remained closed for years.

These who fear the advances of Rome have some grounds for their uneasiness in Glasgow. Roughly one-third of the children in Glasgow schools are Catholics and the great majority of these are regular Sunday church attenders. The percentage of population among adults is not so high, but it is rising steadily, and the number of Catholic adults who attend church on Sunday is much greater than the total for all the Protestant churches put together.

The Catholic growth is a source of uneasiness which flares up now and again into angry and excited agitation, when men who have not darkened a church door for fifty years swear that the Protestant traditions of Scotland must be protected by some means which has not yet been discovered.

From time to time, also, the Church of Scotland investigates the problem and scents out a Catholic plot to secure a dominant position in Scottish life. These efforts have their own flavour of irony. The Church of Scotland itself exercises an influence in public life far in excess of its membership. The public influence of the Catholic Church is far less than its effective membership might warrant. The number of Catholics in important official positions is very small indeed. Nearly all Catholics vote Labour, but very few Catholics are prominent or influential in the Party. James Maxton was a professed atheist, but his Parliamentary seat of Bridgeton was safe as the Rock of Gibraltar, partly because the large Catholic electorate voted for him to a man. (The Orange voters voted solidly against him.)

The interventions of the Catholic Church in local or national politics are sporadic and usually negative. One intervention was decisive. In the years between the Wars a body called the Scottish Protestant League sprang up and made spectacular progress. The Scottish Protestant League insisted that the Catholic Church was a thoroughly evil and corrupting influence and also insisted that the Corporation of Glasgow was in a rotten state. A surprising number of citizens thought there was much to be said for the first theory and everything for the second, and the League captured Council seats both from Socialists and anti-Socialists. For a time it looked like becoming a very serious and dangerous Third Force in municipal politics, and the anti-Socialist Party made the enormous mistake of reaching some kind of understanding with the League for electoral purposes. This understanding cost them their majority on the Town Council and gave the Socialists a long run of office. The Protestant League itself broke up with a good deal of recrimination, and faded almost completely from public view when its leader persisted in proclaiming his affection for Herr Adolf Hitler long after the second World War began. In any event, his "Movement" was too feverish to last.

The demonstration of Catholic voting strength and loyalty was by no means complete. An exceptionally high percentage of Catholics went to the polls because their Church was threatened, but they voted according to their political predilections. If Labour had reached an understanding with the Protestant Alliance, it is by no means certain that the Catholics would or could have defeated them. During the Spanish Civil War, many Socialists lost their customary caution and adopted an attitude that was implicitly anti-Catholic, but they suffered no loss of Catholic support.

In fact, the Catholic Church is so far out of the main stream of Glasgow life that most non-Catholics know very little about it. Catholic news seldom appears in the secular newspapers and when it does, it is very scantily reported. Last year, the *Glasgow Herald* recorded the appointment of a new Archbishop of Edinburgh in two or three inconspicuous lines of small print, much as it might record the appointment of a new bank manager somewhere to some country branch or the golden jubilee of some ancient but obscure minister.

If the strength and the weaknesses of the Catholic community were better known, it would not be so easy for religious dervishes to appeal to ancestral suspicions. But in fact there is little positive interest in the Catholic Church. Catholics claim that they are the authentic

Church of Scotland, but the claim is not even considered by the great majority. However, it is impossible to consider the Catholic Church purely under the heading of religion. Race, economics, criminal statistics, public hygiene and Association football all come into the picture which must be considered in a separate chapter.

To summarize, authority lies with the Established Kirk, fashion and cultural pretensions with the Episcopal Church and the strong point of the Catholic Church is numbers of faithful worshippers. There is a scatter of tiny and lonely sects, each claiming to be the true inheritors of Knox and making of necessity heavy demands on their members, particularly their clergy. General interest in religion is much greater than enthusiasm for practice. This fact is shown now and again in odd ways. For example at the Empire Exhibition of 1938 the Scottish T.U.C. had an exhibit that was not much bigger than a tobacco kiosk, while there were three large and expensive buildings devoted to religion and several smaller exhibits. This by no means indicated the relative importance of religion and Trade Unionism in the life of Glasgow, but it was at least a reminder that the importance of religion was, and is, much greater than church attendance figures would suggest. The Glasgow man's interest may not always be warmly enthusiastic, but it is there. Many of the bleak and ponderous churches may stand almost empty, but they are not ignored. Religion is not treated with amiable indifference, like his London brother. The Glasgow man is not indifferent to religion. Neither, it must be confessed, is he particularly amiable.

CHAPTER EIGHT

EDUCATION

NOWHERE is the democratic nature of the Glasgow community more clearly shown than in the field of education. A tiny proportion of the children go to private schools in the City, and a much tinier proportion go to boarding schools outside, some of them to England. But their numbers are so small that they are hardly noticed, and in educational discussion, the private sector is frequently ignored entirely, and that not through hostility but simply because it is easily overlooked.

The almost universal course for a Glasgow child is to make his start in schooling by toddling off to the primary school round the corner, and to go on from there to the nearest "Secondary". There are one or two good girls' private secondary schools, and there is Glasgow Academy, a private school, for boys. This school educated Sir James Barrie, James Bridie, Jack Buchanan and Baird, the ill-advised inventor of television. It is a good school, if faintly Anglicized, and it shines, if rather modestly, in the nebula of "Public" schools. Nobody in England really knows what a Public School is, and hardly anybody in Glasgow cares. So far as Glasgow is concerned, recognition by the Headmasters' Conference is a straw in the wind or a feather on the scale as compared with massive production of Leaving Certificates or success in the Association or Rugby Football fields.

By much the most famous Glasgow school is the High

School which claims a life of more than eight centuries and is the oldest institution in Glasgow, still fulfilling the purpose for which it was founded. The best girls' school is the Girls' High. They are both Council schools, but Boys' High feels not the faintest inferiority to the privately-owned Academy, nor Girls' High to the privately-owned Park School.

The only social division in the Council schools is between the "High" schools and the ordinary Secondary schools. There are fees in the High schools, of varying amounts, but in none do the fees come near meeting the total cost. There are several private schools which are in a kind of satellite relationship to the Town Council. They are independent, but they are forced to accept some help, or at least a guarantee against loss, from the Council, and they have a Council representative on their Board of Governors. The best-known of these is Hutcheson's Grammar, where John Buchan was a pupil.

But the great majority of parents are perfectly happy to send their children to schools that are as much Council property as the Glasgow trams. It simply does not occur to them that there is any necessary inferiority in a Council education, much less a social stigma attaching to it. Their children may miss certain social nuances and largely escape the mysterious process of character-training, but the parents are happily unaware of the fact.

Indeed, they are a good deal too complacent about Glasgow education. They believe, quite wrongly, that it is in all respects better than anything that England can provide, but there are Council Secondary schools in England from which their Glasgow counterparts could learn a thing or two with advantage.

The primary education is thorough. There is still in Glasgow a lingering suspicion that a child who can spell his own name correctly is somewhat more literate than the child who cannot. There is also a stubborn belief that instructional visits to the local gas works or sewage farm are less useful as a preparation for adult life than a knowledge of the multiplication table. As a result of these obstinate prejudices, quite a high percentage of Glasgow schoolchildren can read and write and count.

School buildings are, on the whole, much better than in England, though some of the slum schools are grim and grimy enough. Playgrounds are nearly always much too small, which is a particular disadvantage in Glasgow where public open spaces are so deplorably few.

The educational standards of the teachers themselves are much above the English. The teachers' training colleges do as good a job as such places can do, and, before the war, it was required of every man who aspired to teach ordinary school subjects that he must have at least a Pass University degree. This rule, which applied to all Scotland, had an unfortunate effect on the Universities, for they were flooded out by men who had just managed to meet the minimum requirements of the Leaving Certificate, still mentally breathing but as exhausted as a Channel swimmer touching the shore at his last gasp. University standards, never very impressive in some of the Arts subjects, inevitably suffered, but at least the rule showed a laudable determination that all children should be taught by teachers who had something to teach. Even under the Emergency Training Scheme, there was very slight relaxation of Scottish standards of qualification. The teachers themselves resisted the dilution which will continue to damage English State education for thirty years or more to come.

If there is not much inclination in Glasgow schools to play with the Play-Way, there is even less inclination to regard a class of young children as a self-governing republic. Discipline is fairly strict, and, much to the distress of educationists, the tawse is not infrequently applied. No doubt this sows the seeds of desperate psychological disasters in adult life, but it keeps the children quiet for the time being, and sometimes makes them do a bit of work.

It must be admitted that in most Glasgow schools, no harm would be done if the human relationship between pupil and teacher were a little warmer. There is plenty of affection shown to the infants, and returned by them, but beyond that stage, the school atmosphere may be bracing, but it is hardly warm.

The Glasgow child is not demonstrative, and in the poorer districts there are too many parents who regard the teacher with something like hostility, or at least with a lack of confidence and friendliness. The teacher is a representative of Authority and is therefore on the other side of the gulf of loyalties.

The atmosphere is considerably warmer in the Catholic schools. This is a trifle surprising, for the Catholic proletariat are even less fond of authority than the non-Catholics who writhe with them beneath the Iron Heel. The explanation may be that the Catholic primary schools are each based on a parish which is a genuine community and has a genuine community sense. It may be that these schools have inherited a warmer educational tradition than the rather severe tradition which is purely Scottish.

It may be that master and pupil in the Catholic school both feel they are members of the same rather isolated minority, and are, therefore, drawn together. Whatever the explanation, the fact is undeniable.

It is a pity that the word "Secondary" no longer has any meaning in the educational vocabulary. It used to mean the education in intellectual subjects given to boys and girls of superior intelligence and industry. This education demanded a reasonable qualification in aptitude and attainment. But the contemporary Secondary education demands no more than that the pupil should have got into his twelfth year without being mentally certified.

The system is a humbug based upon a nonsense, and it is greatly to be regretted that Glasgow should have outpaced even London in its zeal for destructive egalitarianism. Glasgow began "multilateral" schools before the War. These are schools which take in all the "eleven plus" pupils of a district, herding together the bright and the dull, the industrious and the lazy, the civilized and the uncivilized. Once inside the school, the pupils are divided into groups called Academic, Commercial, Technical and so on. Those with the lowest intelligence are called the "C" stream. It is ridiculous to call the best of these Secondary. It is flattery to call the worst of them primary: they are more like Primates. I once set an amateur and strictly unofficial examination to a considerable number of "C" entrants to a multilateral school. The pupils were asked to write down, with correct spelling, their own names, the name of the school they came from, the name of the school they were entering, the name of the street in which that school was situated and the name of the street in which they lived. I was gratified to discover that nearly, though not quite all, could spell their own names, but quite a number found the other questions too hard for them.

The multilateral school is a monstrosity, and it seems strange that it should ever have won approval in Glasgow where education is taken in a serious and severely practical spirit, and where there is a traditional partiality for the clever and hard-working lad. But the system has been introduced in the unholy name of equality. It was introduced because most of the politically active teachers and alleged educationists in Glasgow are Socialists, and Socialists of a particularly sterile and pedantic type.

Glasgow Town Council had a Socialist majority when the multilateral schools were instituted and, during the War, that majority attempted to murder the High School. There is no other word to describe this project.

Glasgow High School has a roll of something more than a thousand pupils. They come from all over Glasgow and from a considerable distance around. They are nearly all the sons of educated parents, and the scholastic record of the school is probably the best in Glasgow. It has other claims to distinction and public respect. It has produced two Prime Ministers in the present century, and the Former Pupils' Rugby Team is generally one of the best in Scotland.

The Socialist Council proposed to make the High School a territorial and multilateral school. That is to say, the school would be compelled to accept all the pupils in a delineated area, and compelled to refuse all pupils outside that area. The mentally lame and halt and blind would come pouring through the gate to gaze with ignorant indifference at the Greek paradigms painted on the class-room wall. The teachers would have to show some versatility of approach. One hour they would be instructing academic pupils in Bradley's Theory of Tragedy, and the next they would be teaching non-academic pupils how to spell "High", and coaxing them on with kindly words of praise to have a shot at spelling "School".

The good scholastic record of the High School is in part explained by the fact that the parents want their boys to learn something, and are willing that they should stay at school until they do. But neither the parents of "C" pupils nor "C" pupils themselves have any such snobbish ambition. The first legal Leaving Day fills the breasts of "C" pupils with delirious joy, and they fly away, unanimously and instantly, like a flock of birds startled by a gun. They run happily into the outside world where nobody will ever ask them to think or to know anything, and where they can earn money, spend their leisure improvingly at the dog races, and vote Socialist, if they can summon up the energy to vote at all. Six or seven hundred of these little fellows would have reduced the High School to a past memory and a present farce. It may be added that the High School is situated in the least populous part of the City, and ten municipal wards had to be allotted to the school to provide enough nitwits to fill the classrooms. Fortunately, this wanton and disastrous proposal was effectively stone-walled by the then Secretary of State, Tom Johnson, himself a Socialist, and in due time the electorate threw the Socialists out.

It is also fortunate that the majority of Glasgow's Secondary Schools are still "unilateral". Any three-quarter-wits who are to be found in them have got there by some mistake and not because of ideology. It is unfortunate that most of the schools are very much too big. The headmaster of a Secondary School with a thousand pupils or more is much in the position of a conductor who cannot see half his orchestra.

Another unfortunate fact is the great wastage of pupils. (This is not true of the *bourgeois* and reactionary High Schools.) A deplorable number of the pupils, including some of the cleverest, leave before they have completed their course. This is explained by one thing only and that thing is free education. Free education is neglected and wasted, just as free milk is neglected and wasted. The absence of even the most modest fees encourages parents to send their children to Secondary Schools, when they have not the faintest intention of keeping them there for one second after the dawn of Liberation Day. If a small sum had to be paid for an expensive education, most of the indifferent parents would send their pupils to the new kind of non-academic Secondary school, where the education rightly costs nothing, for that is what it is worth. The minority who were willing to make the financial sacrifice demanded would begin to take an irascible interest in the amount of homework done.

There are, of course, many intelligent and earnest pupils in Glasgow's Secondary Schools. They are thoroughly and conscientiously taught by teachers of very respectable qualifications. For example, Glasgow, along with the rest of Scotland, positively insists that its teachers of French must be able to speak French and to speak it in such a manner as not to compel a listening Frenchman to stick his fingers in his ears. To that end, it is required that every Honours graduate should teach for a year in France before he enters Training College, to be taught how to teach French.

It is arguable that the pupils are called upon to study too many subjects right through the school. It would be unfair to say that they only get a smattering of many subjects. They get a solid enough grounding, but they cannot possibly get much more. The specialisation of the English system is unknown in Scotland. England possibly carries specialisation too far, or starts it rather too early. (By a happy coincidence, the index to the Spens Report lists "Specialisation (Premature)" immediately before "Spinal Curvature".) On the other hand, Scotland errs grievously in the other direction. The pupil who gets a nap-hand of "Highers" is thought to have done respectably well, but true admiration is reserved to the youth who captures seven or eight "Highers". He is thought to be a budding Aristotle, whereas he is only in a fair way to becoming a journalist.

There is much to be said for instituting "Distinction" in the Leaving Certificate, to be taken a year after the sitting of the Certificate on the ordinary standard. This would reduce the prestige of mere numbers of passes and would also keep University aspirants another year at school, which would be good for them, and much better for the University.

But examination worship is much too prevalent in Glasgow schools. "Play up, play up and play the game" is a cry that rings with but faint appeal in the ears of teachers and parents, if the gallant player is putting up a poor score in Commercial Geography or Dynamics. The amount of homework demanded of the older pupils is onerous indeed, and leaves little time for those intangible elements in education on which the English set such store. It may also explain why moist-eyed enthusiasm for the Old School is not often to be found among Glasgow men. They look back on their old school with respect, and possibly with gratitude for a job of teaching well done, but seldom with warm affection.

Secondary teaching is safe and solid but it is not usually inspiring, and almost never refreshingly eccentric. A few unusual characters recruited from the outside world would do a power of good, but they would not be welcomed. The education authorities, like many other authorities in Glasgow, think they have got all they need within their own solid and slightly stolid ranks. They are wrong.

A man like Elam of Saint Paul's may or may not have been a good teacher, but at least he gave his boys something to talk about in after life, and a glimpse into strange worlds of character and fancy. He would not have lasted long in the service of Glasgow Corporation. When his Headmaster and arch-enemy Walker applied for Saint Paul's, one of the interviewers asked him to describe his teaching methods. After a moment's thought, Walker said, "I walk up and down—like this." He was appointed. Before Glasgow Education Committee he would have been asked to walk out—through the door.

The word "mediocrity" cannot be applied with any fairness to Glasgow Secondary teaching. Good Plus would be a more accurate description, and Very Good Minus more accurate still. But why the minus?

One reason is the unattractiveness of teaching conditions. The salaries paid in Glasgow are now precisely the same as the salaries paid in country districts. This piece of egalitarianism results, typically enough, in a marked inequality. In the days when Glasgow paid a considerably higher salary-scale than the national average, men and women from neighbouring counties were tempted to apply for a Glasgow appointment. Now, there is no temptation, but rather the reverse. A teacher in a country school is better-off in every respect than his Glasgow colleague. He is a more important man in his own community, his classes are smaller, his chances of promotion are much greater, he has no housing difficulties, and he finds the cost of living agreeably low.

The difficulty and chanciness of promotion is the biggest "disincentive" to teaching in Glasgow. Because the schools are large, the number of responsible posts is small. A man may be interviewed for the first modest step up the ladder at the age of fifty-five. This means that headmasterships are often conferred on tottering old gentlemen with one foot already in the Superannuation Scheme. It also means that many women are never considered for promotion at all.

But the greatest grievance is the method of promotion. The Education Committee of Glasgow Corporation has to consider the claims of something like six thousand teachers. Even if the Committee members were competent to assess teaching merit and scholarly qualifications, the numbers of applicants would defeat them. It has happened that a teacher called for interview has had to wait five or six hours in a queue before he was given his chance to proclaim his merits and explain his achievements—in three minutes by the clock. The best Committee in the world must rely very much on guesswork and surface appearances in such conditions.

But Glasgow Education Committee is not the best in the world. Sometimes promotion is granted on grounds of obvious and outstanding merit, but sometimes by influence and favour. It happens, more often than is good for morale, that the worst candidate is chosen. The best teacher is the worst courtier.

It is a sad but undeniable fact that an assembly elected to control municipal transport, sewage and Parish relief is not competent to handle education. The arts which win the popular franchise in local government do not qualify a man to be a judge of a teacher of Greek or the calculus. Education should always and everywhere be controlled by educated men. In Glasgow this is not so.

Between the Education Committee and the teachers stands "The Office", always known as "One Two Nine" from the street number of the building in Bath Street. For a bureaucracy, "The Office" does very well. In matters of sick and compassionate leave, it does very well indeed, and perhaps too well. It shows a highly Christian quality of tolerance for incompetent and cantankerous teachers.

But "The Office" remains a bureaucracy, however well-intentioned the bureaucrats may be. There is a steady and deadening pressure towards uniformity, a multiplication of almost senseless paper work, and a steady diminution of the initiative and authority of the headmaster. Glasgow Corporation schools would be much improved if they were faced with the rivalry of a considerable number of private schools of good standing. In this respect, Edinburgh undoubtedly has a heavy advantage over Glasgow.

The majority of Glasgow teachers lay an almost exclusive emphasis on examination success, and the amount of homework demanded of the older pupils in Secondary schools is almost inhuman. The effect on the boys is modified by the fact that boys will seldom do more than they feel inclined to do, but the leaving examination is a Minotaur which devours a large tribute of maidens, year by year. There is nothing more numbing to the mind and devitalizing to the spirit than excessive study in early years. That is why so many Glasgow girls quietly or hysterically fade out before their course is completed, and why boys who win eight "Highers" and as many first prizes in class, have their brief hour of glory on Prize-Giving Day and are never heard of again. Secondary education in Glasgow is too grimly determined by examination success.

Attempts are made by "educationists" and even by some of the teachers to modify the exclusive interest in paper Certificates, but these attempts are usually foiled by ambitious parents. The ancient and honourable Scottish tradition of pride in academic achievement has always been marred by an undue emphasis on competitive success. That is still regrettably true to-day. Signs of originality or eccentric ability are doubtfully recognized, and whole-hearted praise is given out only to a high total of examination marks. There is little disposition to allow talent to lie fallow for a year or two. The pupil is pushed forward and upwards. The cry is always "Excelsior" and the strange device is ninety-nine per cent in as many subjects as can be squeezed into the school day. It is most especially important that the promising youth should score an average of at least one half of one per cent more than the promising youth next door.

That is not to say that Glasgow people have no respect for education for its own sake. At all levels of society, they have a deep and sincere respect for education as an end in itself. During the Spanish Civil War, there was a most violent and noisy meeting held in Glasgow in support of General Franco. Whenever the speakers referred to any well-known political or social leader who favoured the cause of the General, there were loud yells of execration and derision, and one or more of the interrupters had to be flung downstairs. But one speaker referred to the opinion of a Professor of Spanish, and even the noisiest listened in silence. They regretted that a Professor was on the wrong side, but he was still a Professor, and his views must be treated with respect.

It might be better if Glasgow had a less serious respect for learning, and it would certainly be better if Glasgow ceased to regard scholastic advancement as a kind of League Table. The hot struggle to be top of the class, to win a Hutcheson Trust Bursary, and to crown the school career by being Dux is hardly compatible with an entirely selfless love of learning. Glasgow schools would be more cheerful places if teachers and pupils took their work a little more easily, and the pupils would learn more of what is truly worth learning.

Glasgow is well supplied with more advanced institutions of studies. It has three Medical Schools, which seems an excessive number. The Saint Mungo's College and the Anderson College cater for dental students as well as medical. They are over-shadowed by the University school but they have an honourable past and a useful present. The Veterinary College survived the withdrawal of the Government grant. Former students of the huge Technical College are to be found all over the world, most of them doing very well for themselves.

The College of Domestic Science is situated conveniently near to the University, and the students are a useful addition to the female dancing strength at University

ART AND THE PEOPLE

dances. They can also learn a good deal about Domestic Science if their inclinations run that way.

The Scottish Academy of Music owes much to the generosity of Sir Daniel Stevenson, and, for all I know to the contrary, its teaching quality is unimpeachable.

The Commercial College also owes much to Sir Daniel Stevenson, not least a strong bias towards the study of Spanish.

The Art School is most nobly housed in a large building overlooking Sauchiehall Street. That school has trained a number of fine painters, but it suffers from dilution. A number of the students are young women with nothing much else to do. A much larger number are young men and women who are studying for a teachers' Certificate. Not for them the lonely garret and the crust of bread. Their minds are fixed on a secure salary, with superannuation rights. Their ambition is respectable and even laudable, but Picasso had different ideas. In its time, Glasgow Art School has made a real impact on painting, and may do so again. However, the greatest benefit which the Art School confers upon Glasgow is its dedication to studies in which nobody can pretend that examination marks have much meaning.

But by far the most important institution of advanced learning is the University. A high place in the Bursary List is the ambition of every school Dux in the West of Scotland. To win the top place is the greatest possible achievement for both school and pupil. It has been known for a brilliant youth who came second or third in the examination to wait for another year and try again to be first. There is no financial advantage in being the Prima Donna Assoluta of the exam, but there is eminent glory. The top marker is the Dux of all the Duxes. He enters the University with the proud, assured step of a conqueror. As like as not, he leaves it to be a Civil servant, with a brief case and a black soft hat, or to acquire chilblains as a junior lecturer in a Canadian University. But, till his dying day, he will never forget the moment when he opened the *Glasgow Herald* to read the results and saw that his name led all the rest. Life has no richer reward for the youth who has been taught that sweetness and light can be measured on a percentage scale.

CHAPTER NINE

THE UNIVERSITY

NO one looking at the University of Glasgow would readily guess that it is five hundred years old. The historic College, in High Street (the scene of the duel in *Rob Roy*) was sold to a railway company in the nineteenth century, and a new building was erected on high ground above Kelvingrove Park.

The site could hardly be bettered, but unfortunately the architectural design was entrusted to Gilbert Scott. This is a permanent grievance among Glasgow æsthetes, who believe that the job should have been given to the local architect, Thompson. Thompson was a more original and no doubt a better architect than Scott, but it is at least doubtful if he was the man best suited to take full advantage of the opportunity and of the site. He severely and justly criticized Scott's design, but it is by no means certain that any effort of his own would have been much of an improvement.

Scott's building, lying along the crest of the hill, has been compared to a liner stranded on a reef. The building is long and uninteresting, and the tower in the middle is a pointless and unimpressive addition. Two pieces of the old High Street College reconstructed on the new site put Scott's building to shame.

That is not to say that Scott's building is offensive. It is not. It is just nothing in particular. But the excellence of the site and the quality of the stone make it enormously superior to, let us say, the dreadful University building in Liverpool. Many additional buildings have been added to the main blocks. These are of varying merit, but the new Reading Room is a genuinely pleasing and distinguished piece of work.

The University has been fortunate in its ability to put up all, or nearly all, the new additions on the same site as the main building, but further additions will leave little space for the easy and gracious living of those students who prefer not to attend their classes. There has been a certain spill-over across University Avenue to the residential district of Hillhead. The streets on the other side of the Avenue consist of large and solid stone houses, mostly of the terrace type, some of them quite handsome. The University has acquired a number of these, but might perhaps have acquired many more in the inter-war years, when they were selling for a beggarly price. The houses went cheaply because their rating valuation was high, by Glasgow standards. As the University does not pay rates, there was good reason for buying up all that came on the market. If that had been done, a beginning would have been made in the creation of a whole University town. These agreeable streets might have been predominantly devoted to tutorial centres, residences for the staff and residential halls for students. The area is self-contained and clearly defined. The University might have owned not merely the ridge, but the whole of Gilmorehill (the hill on which it stands) and Glasgow would have been the richer for a secluded area of light and learning where hardly anybody needed to worry about rent and rates.

That opportunity was lost, and is not likely to return

for many years. The University grounds now carry more buildings than is agreeable. A feeling of space is a spiritual necessity to the student who is disinclined to do any work. The space is no longer there, except in front where the steep grass slope that runs down to Kelvingrove Park still provides pleasant sleeping accommodation on a warm Summer's afternoon.

For the visitor, by much the most interesting part of the University is the Hunterian Museum. This houses the extraordinary collection left by Hunter, the great surgical pioneer. It is a mixed collection. Stuffed South American moths and butterflies, fine examples of protective colouration, are interesting in themselves, but are not the most appropriate companions for an unusually good collection of Greek coins. There is a handful of Rembrandts, one of them superb, which distract the eye from a large piece of stone which bends if you lean on it. In the variety of kind and quality of its exhibits, the Hunterian is rather like a good old-fashioned Museum in a County town, but its rarest possessions are rare indeed. It is a memorial to a great man of extraordinary enterprise and versatility in taste and curiosity. A visitor to Glasgow with an afternoon to spare could spend it very pleasantly in the Hunterian. If he also felt energetic, he could climb the University tower, that is impressive in nothing but height and yet gives an exhilarating view of Glasgow and the river.

There are many niches in the walls of the main building. They are not good niches, as niches go, and they look none the better for being empty. As the Presbyterian faith is so emphatically disapproving of the worship of Saints, it must be presumed that the niches were intended to hold statues of the men who have added lustre to the University throughout the ages. Considering the quality of the statues in George Square and Kelvingrove Park, the University may have shown prudence and sagacity in leaving them empty, but something should be done to remind students of their inheritance.

No University worthy of the name can exist for five centuries without making a considerable impact on the world. Glasgow University's great age began with the last quarter of the eighteenth century when Watt was working at his steam engine and Professor Adam Smith was literally telling the world about the origin of the Wealth of Nations. Seldom has any University given house-room to such a formidable pair. Hunter, who has been called the father of modern surgery, belonged to the same time which also saw the beginnings of the Glasgow philosophical tradition.

Those were indeed the days, the days when the University could afford to turn down Edmund Burke for a Chair because they considered that the local boy, Adam Smith, was more suitable. Glasgow, along with the other Scottish Universities, enjoyed a considerable prestige among the censorious in England as well as in Scotland because of the slack moral standards and unimpressive scholarship of Oxford and Cambridge. (It should be noted that James Boswell was one of Glasgow's upright, industrious and God-fearing undergraduates.) Something was also owing to the Thirty-nine Articles and the Anglican Establishment which closed the ancient English Universities to Dissenting students and sent some of them North to win a non-Erastian and unsuperstitious degree. (Amongst the young men who came to Glasgow for moral and mental improvement was Melbourne, but he was a Dissenter, not in a theological, but in an alarmingly wide sense.) Ireland also sent a considerable number of its Dissenting sons, Hazlitt's father among them. To the present day a trickle of Welsh students comes to study philosophy in Glasgow, and Wales has given much more than its appropriate quota of philosophy teachers.

These relative advantages were lost in the nineteenth century. When Oxford and Cambridge decided, or were told, to do some work, they rapidly regained their pre-eminent prestige, and when they opened their gates to Dissenters, they had, at least for students of the liberal arts, something to offer with which the Scottish Universities could hardly compete.

Before this happened, a start had been made with the foundation of regional Universities in England, based largely on the Scottish model. Indeed, Thomas Campbell the Glasgow poet played an enthusiastic and leading part in the foundation of London University. He was an ardent and forcible spirit who was immensely popular among Glasgow students. They elected him Lord Rector three times, in defiance of the University Senate, and to this day they commemorate this triumph over the reactionary greybeards by singing Campbell's song "Ye mariners of England" at the beginning of classes. It is not a self-evidently appropriate song for a Scottish University, and it would be interesting to learn just how many Glasgow students know why they sing it.

In one respect, Glasgow University is markedly different from London and the other nineteenth-century creations. London was undenominational. This is the result of the deep disagreements between the Anglicans and Dissenters. Wellington had expressed himself willing to have two faculties of Theology, but there was a general agreement that there was something not quite right in this compromise, something like having a Chair of Astronomy and another of Astrology.

In Glasgow, by contrast, theology retained its formal paramountcy for a long time. It was taken for granted that the Principal of the University must be a Presbyterian divine, the leading philosophers were also divines, and the school of divinity produced men who played an important part in Church life, not only in Scotland but also in the Dominions and the United States.

But as the nineteenth century came to its end and the twentieth began, the balance tilted slowly but surely against divinity and even against the liberal arts, in favour of more practical subjects. It was in engineering, and medicine, and to a lesser degree, science, that Glasgow maintained truly international standards. The Chairs of Humane Studies were often enough occupied by men of great eminence, but the students of these subjects were, and are, notably less advanced than the students of Oxford and Cambridge.

If proof of this inferiority were needed, it would be found in the fact that the Blue Ribbon of the Arts Faculty in Glasgow is the Snell Scholarship which entitles the winner to spend four years in Balliol. Leaving Glasgow with a First, he starts again in Oxford as an undergraduate.

This state of affairs cannot be called satisfactory, and it might be considerably improved by some simple reforms. The brilliant youth who tops the Bursary

Competition in half a dozen subjects has undoubtedly laid an imposing foundation for a general education, and he has none of the weaknesses of some brilliant English-taught lads whose startling proficiency in one line is matched by an equally startling ignorance everywhere else. But if the Scottish all-rounder went straight to Oxford or Cambridge, he would find himself starting a long way behind scratch, if he took an Honours course in, say, classics or history. He could give his rival points in a whole range of other subjects, but he would take a pretty severe beating in any one school. A post-Certificate year of rigid specialisation would improve his standards greatly and would also send him to the University a year older, which would be highly desirable from every point of view.

Another practicable though expensive improvement would be the special treatment of Honours students from the start of their course. At one time, the subjects that the students for an ordinary degree had to take were rigidly fixed. There is now a considerable latitude of choice, but it is not absolute. The man who wants to dodge Logic must take Moral Philosophy instead. Mathematics may be avoided, but at the cost of something else that may be almost equally unpalatable. There is much to be said for this restriction of choice, for at least it prevents ordinary students from prowling round the curriculum picking out soft subjects, like a cat picking tit-bits out of a dustbin. But it has this disadvantage that any ordinary class has a proportion of students who are there not because they have any interest in the subject but because they think it is easy, or, at least, is not quite so difficult as the only possible alternative. These students are lazy or generally not very bright, or are bright enough but have no aptitude for this particular subject. Even if the classes were small it would be difficult for the teachers to create a lively intellectual tone when a fair number of their students have no spontaneous interest in what they are being taught, and have no higher ambition than to struggle through to a minimum pass mark.

But many of the classes are very large indeed. At one time the ordinary English class had over six hundred students, and was held in two sessions, like a variety show. This monstrous growth was exceptional and temporary, but in the more important subjects (important for Degree purposes) the roll is still counted in hundreds. That is one reason why the standard cannot be high and why individual attention is so scanty. A former Professor of History proudly claimed that he endeavoured to speak to every one of his Ordinary students at least once a year, even if it was only to say "Good morning". As he has several hundred students in his class, even this modest standard of personal communication demanded a considerable effort, a greater effort than some Professors are inclined to make, but it still did not amount to much.

The student who declares himself for Honours should be called upon to pass the Ordinary and the Higher Ordinary examinations on a much sterner standard than the pass student. This is already done with students who are aiming at the higher degree in Law, and it would compel Honours students to do some serious work from the word "go".

Honours students should also be given serious tutorial attention from the start. This would not be possible without increasing the size of the present staff, which is already

9

badly overworked, while doing a barely decent minimum of tutorial work. Money for unspectacular reforms of this kind is hard to come by, but truly enlightened donors could not dispose of their money better than by founding teaching scholarships for young graduates of high quality who could earn while they learn by doing tutorial work at the same time as they are studying for a higher degree. It would be no bad thing if the students had to pay a modest fee for their tutorial instruction.

So long as the present system continues, the progress made even by the best students will be less impressive than the undoubtedly high quality of many of their instructors would lead one to expect. Some of the greatest of the University's scholars have felt very uneasy at the remoteness of contact with their students, which the size of their classes lays upon them. After all, Socrates would not have been particularly influential if he had never said more than a hasty "good morning" to Thrasymachus and the other Doctor Watsons of his entourage.

The Law Faculty merges into Arts, for the students trying for an LL.B must first take an Arts degree. Law classes are timed to suit office hours, with the result that legal students flit through the University like forpinéd ghosts. They are creatures of grey dawns and gloomy twilights, patrons of workmen's transport and victims of the evening rush hour.

The Medical Faculty has a glorious tradition and it offers a conscientious, thorough and sensible course of training, but it is difficult to avoid the suspicion that, for the moment, it is rather lacking in teachers of outstanding eminence. It is not reasonable to demand a Lister in every generation of teachers, but twenty years ago, Sir

Robert Muir ("Bobby") ruled the whole world of Pathology and Sir William McEwan was King of Surgery. Are there any royal personages in the Faculty to-day? (McEwan once addressed the British Association and ended his speech with the passionate and electrifying declaration: "Periosteum never has become, and never can become, osteoblast." The Duke of Windsor, then Prince of Wales, was President for that year. It was observed that this outburst of eloquence left him strangely unmoved.)

If it is true, as many doctors believe, that the Medical Faculty of Glasgow has sunk into a respectable rut, then one of the glories of the University is eclipsed, let us hope only temporarily. A bright respectable average standard is simply not good enough for a school with such a glittering history. What is badly needed is a handful of teachers with a truly international reputation. The Medical Faculty should be out in the world, like the manager of a football team, buying talent. A comfortable place in the Second Division is not to be contemplated.

The Science Faculty suffers from the same disadvantage as Arts, though in a lesser degree, but Glasgow is now going in for science in a big way. In the present deplorable age, there is not much difficulty in getting buckets of money for scientific research, both from public and from private sources, and no difficulty at all if the research is devoted to finding a method of blowing the whole world to bits in one smoothly conceived explosion. The inhumanities now occupy the commanding prestige and influence once occupied by theology.

This is unfortunate, to put it mildly. Even in an age less obsessed with the exploration of disastrous techniques,

Glasgow found it difficult to maintain the prestige of the ivory tower against the growing assertiveness of the scientific pre-fab. Now, the balance is shifting everywhere against the disinterested study of entirely useless subjects. The patrons of the new black arts expect strictly practical results, at least in the long term. The ascendancy of science is the ascendancy of materialism. This is not always and necessarily true, but it is true in the dismal conditions of the present age. What Glasgow University needs is a large endowment, innocent of strings, to be used to redress the balance now tilting so heavily in favour of the scientific disciplines. Divinity has lost almost all of its former prestige, and if humane studies shrink even more timidly into the shades, no triumphs in atomic anarchy, heat engines or even in medicine will preserve the status of the University as an authentic *studium generale*. The problem is not the less urgent because it is by no means singular to Glasgow.

Of Divinity, there is little that can be said by a layman who is not a Presbyterian. The days are gone when it was taken for granted that the Principal must be a Divinity man. It is a still farther cry to the days when a Principal like Patrick Gillespie was an architect of Scottish history. Doubtless there are still learned and distinguished men in the Faculty, but they have no obvious impact on the life of the University. The divines still enjoy a high formal precedence but their influence has most sadly shrunk.

Those who should know maintain that the Faculty of Engineering is in the healthiest state of all. This is scarcely surprising, for Glasgow is well supplied with people of deep engineering knowledge and critical standards. The Faculty had better be good. It is good. So all is well.

Student life in Glasgow is markedly different from student life in the ancient English Universities, and also different, though not so markedly, from student life in the English provincial Universities. There are hardly any rules to govern the life of the Glasgow student and there are no proctors to enforce the few rules that there are. On the first day of his arrival at the University, the student is dropped in at the deep end and left to sink or swim. All the "Don'ts" he is called upon to respect are painted on a single notice board, with a good deal of room for other matter. If he takes the wrong turning, months and even years may pass before anybody notices the fact.

The tradition of Glasgow University is a tradition of students who live meagrely and turn their hands to any work that will pay their fees and modest lodging costs. The tradition survives although it is now true only of a minority. Government and Council subsidies have opened the gates of the University to all the deserving and to some of the undeserving.

Few students maintain themselves entirely by their own efforts, but a very large number do some profitable work, mostly during vacations, and are not entirely amenable to the most kindly tutelage. Many years ago, Yeats gave a speech in the Union, when he dismissed University students as young men and women totally out of contact with the hard realities of life. He was surprised when the audience vigorously rejected the idea that they belonged to the *jeunesse doree*. Among the audience was a young student of Arts who spent half the year as a working miner. There were others who passed the Summer as pursers on Clyde steamers or made money playing the saxophone in jazz bands, not to mention the engineering students who spent half their year working side by side with toilers in the yards of the Clyde and further afield. Not all the students who do part-time or occasional work are under economic necessity to do so. They are members of a University which is very close to the economic earth, and they do an occasional job of work because they like it. Also, they can use the money.

"Meal Monday" commemorates an age of even plainer living and conceivably higher thinking. In the days before Welfare hung like a benignant rainbow over the Highland hills, one Monday in every term was a classless day, when country students brought back a bag of meal from the family croft, walking all the way. Legends of Glasgow students are legends of devoted young men who won the highest distinctions in circumstances of dire poverty, and often died as the feeble and fevered hand was stretched out to receive the prize. The Glasgow Grammarian's Funeral sometimes anticipated his graduation.

There is much that is noble and austere in the tradition, but it is distorted and abused by those modern students who take a pugnaciously self-righteous pride in refusing to play any part in University social life. It is difficult to understand why these young men are self-righteous, for they do not trim the lamp of scholarship with any zeal for lonely and disinterested study. All they want is a degree that will guarantee them a State-paid job, with superannuation comfortably and consolingly attached. This is perhaps very natural, but it is hard to see why it should be considered meritorious. The Glasgow men

who have made a mark of distinction in the world of
scholarship and active affairs have almost all been men
who wasted some time in social life and were all the
better and wiser for it.

The tradition of austerity has another disadvantage,
for it includes a tradition of roughness. That is not to
say that Glasgow students have hooligan tendencies.
There is hardly any conflict between Town and Gown,
which is not surprising considering that the University
is Town with a Gown on. Glasgow students do not think
it funny to break windows or run down a street overturn-
ing bicycles.

On the other hand, they are ungentle with lecturers and
professors. The custom of opening a lecture with boisterous song, sometimes impressively delivered, is very well.
But it is not so well when the singing goes on all through
the hour of instruction, and the teacher welcomes the bell
of dismissal as fervently as a boxer at the end of a gruelling
round.

A solid hour of community singing is not the usual
routine, but it happens, or it did happen, rather too often.
This is surely inadvisable, even from the utilitarian point
of view, in a University where the class lecture plays a
dominant part. The great Kelvin was admittedly a highly
incompetent teacher. In vain did he demonstrate the
discoveries of Faraday by means of the instruments used
by Faraday himself when his class was in no mood to
listen.

When Kelvin, then plain Mr. Thompson, went off to
lay the Atlantic cable, his place was taken by a Mr. Day,
much inferior in scientific genius, but much superior as a
teacher. Just before the great man came back, burdened

with celebrity and a brand-new knighthood, a student wrote on the blackboard, "Work while the Day liveth, for the Knight cometh wherein no man may work."

The pun was ingenious, but the fact remains that the men could have worked under the Knight if they had been disposed to listen. Not all Glasgow teachers are so ineffective as Kelvin. The late and great John Phillimore silenced rowdiness for once and for all by pausing in his lecture to say, "Gentlemen, I have some more pearls." It is creditable to the Glasgow student community, and also characteristic, that the men who were the subjects of this rebuke were the first to appreciate it, with unforced and ingenuous admiration. The late Professor Gregory was not an obviously magnetic personality, and no one except a geologist would describe Geology as a subject calculated to grasp the student soul with bonds of steel. Yet Gregory had no difficulty in holding his class in a state of docile incomprehension. This effortless mastery is not plausibly explained by the fact that Gregory's reputation was far-stretching, for Kelvin's reputation stretched further than the Atlantic cable and his classes yet resembled a disorderly political meeting. Gregory commanded respect because he was the scholar who was also a man of action. What student could fail to warm to a man like Gregory? He sat up half the night failing most of the examinees, and set off next morning for China. Then, in a tour of exploration, he fell over a cliff and was found and rescued only because the luminous dial of his wristlet watch told the rest of the party where he was hanging on a bush. He returned just in time to correct the next examination and fail most of his students once again. In the end, Gregory was drowned in the Orinoco. The

great MacEwan preserved total order in his class, probably by the authority of his majestic frown, and partly by
the fact that his class was small and it was easy to detect
disturbers of the academic peace. Ritchie Girvan, the
specialist in Old English, not only imposed himself on his
class, but on the whole University. Engineering students,
at the other and darker end of the intellectual spectrum,
knew Ritchie Girvan and loved him respectfully from afar.

These are only a few of the men who found no difficulty
in controlling their classes, in a particularly rumbustious
generation. But they all had some exceptional authority
or teaching talent, and that is more than can be demanded
of every aspirant to a University teaching post. Glasgow
students expect (or used to expect) to be wooed and won,
with the result that diffident suitors have a rough time, and
more cautious gentlemen firmly decline a Glasgow
appointment.

This is a real loss to Glasgow University and the loss is
probably more important now than it was fifty years ago.
Apart from the provincial Universities of England, a
variety of cultural and research organizations sponsored
by the Government or by simple-minded philanthropists
offer the young scholar a decent competence for no greater
effort than remaining conscious for a modest proportion
of the hours of the week. Men who can procure one of
the jobs which are the contemporary equivalent of a
chantry priest's will not be tempted to take a Glasgow
appointment, unless they have a genuine zeal for teaching
and a taste for a battle of personalities and wills.

However, the Scottish educational tradition has always
been boisterous. When Walter Scott was a schoolboy,
youngsters of respectable and even of notable families

engaged in stone-throwing gang fights of a ferocity that would gravely disturb a Delinquent Court to-day. With such a tradition, it is not to be expected that Scottish students will preserve a church-like atmosphere in the classroom. If the teacher fails to hold their attention, the loss is the teacher's and also the students'. The outside world is not much concerned.

It is different when a visiting speaker is expected to engage in mental and spiritual all-in wrestling with the audience which listens (or does not listen) to him. Having the highest respect for every ancient custom, I still could not see, even in my student days, why distinguished men invited to Glasgow University Union should not be accorded the elementary civilities which may well be demanded by all guests, and demanded with some asperity by guests who are doing their hosts a favour. The late Lord Horne, himself a Glasgow graduate, once suffered not very witty but continued interruptions in the Union for a few minutes, and then walked off the platform with a parting message of benevolent good will. I thought he had a firm grasp of the right idea.

An exception must be made for speakers in Rectorial contests. If they do not know what to expect, somebody should take them aside beforehand and tell them the facts of Glasgow University Life. The election of the Lord Rector is an occasion for the most exhilarating rowdiness. The supporters of the rival candidates have not yet got round to using atomic weapons, but they make quite an impressive row without the aid of nuclear science. A prominent zealot for one candidate may find himself snatched by zealots for another candidate and shut up in a remote Highland cottage or dumped on a whaler headed for the Polar regions. Parents have been known to express some anxiety and a hint of irritation when their sons disappear suddenly from human knowledge, but such unsporting peevishness should be firmly discouraged. The tradition of kidnapping, of mock battle, of assaults on enemy headquarters and of hot-foot pursuits through the streets is a noble tradition. A Rectorial election is a Carnival with knuckle-dusters.

People who come to speak in Rectorial campaigns have sometimes found the experience disconcerting. The point and purport of a neatly-turned epigram is apt to be lost when a bag of flour is emptied over the epigrammatist's head. But a Rectorial is a free-for-all, with no respect for persons, and if the celebrated speakers do not know what to expect, they learn very soon, and they learn the hard way.

The culmination of the contest is the Rectorial fight on voting day. This is an excellent affair. Bags of soot, fish-heads and rotten eggs (if any) are freely employed. The parties fight for possession of the door to the polling place. In better days, the party which won the battle could be expected, with some confidence, to win the election as well, but that is no longer true. At a prearranged time, the battle comes to an end, and then the women students walk in, unmolested, to cast an almost unanimous vote for the least interesting of the candidates. There may be something to be said for Universities of mixed sex, but not much, and what it may be is yet to be discovered.

The violence and the vigour of a Rectorial contest are altogether admirable, but there is nothing at all to be said for the modern heresy of carrying the violence over to the Rectorial Address. Normally, the Lord Rector's duties begin and end with the Address, and it seems only fair and proper that the Address should be heard. But the most recent Rectorial Address became the occasion for an insensate brawl which gained unhelpful headlines in at least two continents.

The Lord Rector could not make himself heard at all, and he was reduced to sheltering from the missiles thrown at him by covering his face with the Rector's gown. He stood like a delinquent in the pillory. If this can be excused as high spirits, then Borstal may claim Collegiate status.

Perhaps fortunately, Rectorials come only once in three years, and normal student life is less exciting. In the world of athletics and games, the standing of Glasgow University is not so high as it might be. In any student generation, a first-class Soccer team could be fielded, if it were not for the fact that the most brilliant Soccer players very sensibly play for professional teams. The Rugby team is also normally unimpressive. In most years, a fully representative Glasgow University Rugby team could meet Oxford and/or Cambridge and be modestly confident of pushing them around. But the best players do not play for the University. They play for their old school Former Pupils' Clubs, and turn out for the University only on rare occasions. The University team has a poor chance against the High School or the Academy Former Pupils, largely because these teams have first call upon so many University men. Even in pure athletics the University cannot always command the support of all the best student performers. Because of this, the students whose homes and old schools are at a healthy distance from Glasgow play a part in the athletic life of the University far more important than their numbers would justify.

It is much the same with the general social life of the University. Students from Glasgow and neighbourhood are numerically an overwhelming majority. Engineering and Medicine attract a number of foreign and Dominion students, and there is a Highland contingent represented in all the Faculties. But the majority of students travel from their homes to the University daily. They have so many local loyalties and interests that they are not easily persuaded to take a full part in University social life.

The students who take the last possible tram to the University and the first possible tram home again may not be in the majority, but they are plentiful enough. They never attend Union Debates, they could hardly find their way to the athletic ground, they are strangers to the Class and Year Societies, and too many of them count their indifference as a virtue.

Nevertheless, it was possible before the War to live a full, satisfying and instructive student life in Glasgow University without spending time in the lecture rooms, except for an occasional courtesy visit. The hours could be fleeted away in a pleasant and improving manner without any assistance or direction from the teaching staff.

Some men, indeed, found the life so pleasant that they remained as students for ten or fifteen years. These were the Chronics. Walter Elliott has written of them in noble and judicious prose. For the most part they were not stupid or even conspicuously lazy men. They simply took a different and more thoughtful view of life than the throngs of youngsters who wasted their youth in foolish striving for examination success. The Chronics did not waste their youth, or even their early middle-age, in such sterile pursuits. They were established figures, well-known and respected by all. In a University with such a strong tradition of non-intervention, nobody reproached them or urged them to plunge with more vigour into the intellectual battle. They smoked their pipes and drank their beer, and discoursed in a sage manner on the manners and morals of the human race and the complexities of the human condition. Advancing years brought them maturity of judgment, and a slow, very slow, accretion of knowledge. A South African Chronic of ripe vintage once sat in a hotel bar, surrounded by fellow students for the medical profession, who did not conceal an unworthy anxiety to get through the course in the minimum time. Suddenly the Chronic pointed to a sleeping cat and asserted himself. "I may have failed my second Professional six times," he declared, "but I know that cat's going to have kittens".

Some Chronics faded away, like old soldiers, which they generally were. Others, having exhausted the patience of their most trusting relatives, turned at last to their books and passed their examinations, not infrequently collecting prizes on the way. Osborne H. Mavor was not a genuine shellback Chronic, but he most conspicuously failed (he did not even try) to run his academic course in evens. Yet, he became a Professor of Medicine, and, under the name of James Bridie, won large fame and rich rewards as a writer of plays.

Most students lacked the strong character and also the solid family background to graduate as Chronics, but any young man of a sociable and enterprising disposition could have a very good time and still move forward with decent speed towards his degree.

Union Debates were good fun. There was little or none of the carefully cultivated whimsicality which marks Union speaking at Oxford and Cambridge. The Glasgow climate is as unfavourable to oratorical nonsense as to all other kinds of nonsense. But the level of speaking was plain and respectable, with a good deal of common-sense, some wit, and strict attention to the subject under discussion. The same unpretentious competence was shown in the speaking at the meetings of political, regional or academic societies.

Smoking concerts and dinners were enlivened by genuinely good comic turns and by some fine singing, especially from Highland students. Glasgow students are agreeably given to song, and when they are massed in some special gathering, the noise they can make is always impressive and sometimes moving.

The most active of the political clubs were the Labour and Nationalist Clubs (the latter being powerfully sustained by men of exceedingly Irish names). The most inactive was the Conservative Club. Except for the Rectorial season, that Club lived in a state of majestic inertia. There was no nonsense about study circles or little research groups. A boisterous smoking concert now and again was all that the Conservatives considered to be necessary in the way of political education. There was almost everything to be said for this point of view.

Interest in the non-political societies is far from steady. A few active spirits may quicken a society like the Dialectic into vigorous life for a few years, only to leave the University and sadly watch a rapid and heavy decline.

The regular contributors to the University Magazine, the *G.U.M.* are an informal community of their own. The *G.U.M.* has a steadier character and a higher average level of success than most of the student institutions. Under the inspiration of John Phillimore and O. H. Mavor, the *G.U.M.* early established a meritorious tradition of light verse which has been maintained with remarkable consistency ever since. Only an unscrupulous propagandist would maintain that any University magazine is good, but the *G.U.M.* is better than the *Isis*, and though it is not good, it has printed a remarkable number of good things, many in verse, not so many in prose, and a few in the way of cartoons and illustrations. Fleet Street is well-stocked with men who first blotted paper for the *G.U.M.*

But it is a strange and disappointing fact that a high proportion of those who show authentic literary promise and sometimes positive achievement do nothing at all with their talent once they graduate. The bowler hat is a very effective extinguisher of the immortal flame. In the city of no nonsense, flights of fancy are not looked on with much favour. A licence is accorded to students, with excellent results, but on graduation day the licence is sharply withdrawn. A chartered accountant who indulges in verse had better have private means.

If much of this is written in the past tense, there is a sad reason. The Ministry which can grant or withhold deferments of military service hangs like a cloud over every student. There is a Cup-Tie atmosphere of strain and nervous worry as examination time comes near. A couple of failures is fatal. Long before any man can qualify even as a novice Chronic, he is whipped away to the barrack square. "The thoughtless day, the easy night" have become part of a past which is rapidly receding, and is even in danger of being forgotten. The Grim Reaper of the Ministry of Labour stands in the background of all festive occasions. The words of "Gaudeamus" now ring out with a double overtone of melancholy. "Nos habebit humus." Yes, indeed. For "humus" read the Ministry of Labour and you have the reason for a sad decline.

CHAPTER TEN

CULTURE

BECAUSE there is no nonsense in Glasgow, there is little talk of culture. Glasgow has none of Manchester's very active consciousness of its own cultural interests. Nor has it any of London's bland unconsciousness of there being any culture anywhere beyond the L.C.C. area, except perhaps in Oxford and Cambridge.

But there are lively intellectual and artistic interests in Glasgow, even although they are not extensively advertised. For a long time, the wealthier Glasgow merchants have maintained a fine tradition of intelligent picture-buying, and Glasgow Art Gallery in Kelvingrove Park has benefited largely from the bequests of men who were not afraid to buy right up to the taste of their time and even beyond it.

The Art Gallery is a curious building. It would be unjust to say that it has no pretensions to beauty. It has many pretensions, but they are all unfounded. The ground floor of this Italianate building houses a worse than mediocre display of statuary, and also an extensive collection of ship models and of rather uninteresting specimens illustrating Natural History. If the whole building were devoted to the display of paintings, it would still be too small, but the ground floor is totally unsuitable for that purpose, a thought which might well have occurred to those who authorized the design.

The picture collection is impressively good in some directions, but rather weak in others. The lack of balance is explained by the bad tradition of the Corporation which sits back and waits for dead men's pictures. This is not good enough, for it means that the development of the Gallery is shaped by dead men's taste. The Corporation does spend some money on pictures, but not much, and, in the past, the money was not always wisely spent.

Fortunately, the present Curator of the Gallery is very much of a professional who learned about modern painting the hard way. But although Dr. Honeyman can be trusted to spend what money comes his way with taste and artistic foresight, his position would be easier if the Art Gallery (and all the other art collections of the City) were not under the control of the Parks Committee of the Town Council.

The logic of this arrangement is simple but unsound. The Art Gallery stands in Kelvingrove Park. Therefore the Committee which looks after tulips, litter collection and old men's shelters must also look after the Manets and the Picassos (if any). The Committee members appear to work on the principle that they don't know much about painting, but they know what they don't like. A Committee responsible for nothing but the Art Collections, heavily strengthened by co-opted members with professional knowledge, would have spent its modest income in a less parochial manner than the actual Committee has done in the past. The parochial spirit of the Committee was amusingly illustrated at the time of the great exhibition of Dutch art at Burlington House. The Hunterian Museum at the Kelvingrove Gallery made a notable contribution to the show, but a Hobbema sent from Kelvingrove was returned with regret, for the good and sufficient reason that it was not by Hobbema. The Committee at once made a noise like an indignant lady who has had cruel doubt cast on the authenticity of her marriage lines. The Committee would have done better to stick to their tulips. Doubtless they understand tulips.

In recent years, Glasgow has received a startling windfall in the Burrell Bequest. For quality and variety, it can have few equals among the most princely collections in the world. Unfortunately, the collection contains fabrics so rare and delicate that they must be housed far away from city smoke, and, again unfortunately, it is not likely that a suitable building will be put up for some years. But when the collection is fully available it will be worth going many miles to see. It is to be hoped that it will have an elevating and instructive effect on the Parks Committee.

Glasgow men take much pride in the fame and achievement of the Glasgow School of Painting which was of some international prominence and importance half a lifetime ago. It is dangerous for the uninstructed layman to dogmatize on questions of art, but I must suggest that the influence of the Glasgow School has been exaggerated by the loyal locals. The painters of the School were widely advertised far beyond Glasgow and some of them, notably Sir John Lavery, made a lot of money. There was a deal of talent and some originality among the enterprising young painters of Glasgow, but was there ever a time when the "throne of Art" in Paris was shaken by the Glasgow onrush? The Glasgow School was an unusually interesting regional development, but was it ever much more? How many of the great men of the school look particularly great to-day? Opinions will differ, but, although I hope to re-visit Glasgow shortly, I will venture the suggestion that, in modern times, Edinburgh has produced more good painters than Glasgow. For a Glasgow man, this is an admission that must wrench the soul.

But, however he may feel about the glories of the past, the most loyal citizen will hardly pretend that Glasgow painting is a major influence in contemporary art. The annual exhibition of the Fine Art Institute is a peaceable affair. It is marked by a decent quality of technical competence, but anyone who considers it in the least degree daring must have been brought up entirely on coloured picture postcards.

There are, of course, painters of quality in Glasgow and there is some brighter promise for the future, but Glasgow at the moment is not one of the important art centres of the world.

There never has been a Glasgow School of literature. Several contemporary Glasgow novelists have been highly successful, but of writers still living or recently dead, only James Bridie can be regarded as a star of the First League. His admirers were exasperated by his stubborn refusal to finish a play in a neat and tidy manner, but this most genially cantankerous of men went his own wilful way and in spite of their irritation his admirers kept on admiring.

James Bridie was by far the brightest ornament of the Citizens' Theatre which encourages native talent and also endeavours to persuade the theatre-going public to pay their money to see plays that the commercial theatre would hardly touch. It is a dispiriting struggle, for Glasgow is by no means given to patronizing unusual ventures on the stage. (Glasgow loves musical comedy with a fervour as single-minded and depressing as its addiction to sausage and chips.) The excellent company of the Citizens can always secure good houses by putting on an Irish play, but the Irish play is seldom remarkable, and, in any event, the Citizens' Theatre is the descendant of the Scottish National Players, and inherits the purpose of promoting Scottish National, not Irish National, drama.

However, if Glasgow is far from distinguished for its intelligent patronage of the professional or half-professional drama, there is something like a mania for acting in amateur production, and there is quite a brisk and profitable local industry in the writing of one-act plays for the host of amateur companies. The plays, like the companies, vary immensely in quality. Nearly the worst are the depressingly sentimental Kailyaird comedies, and it is painful to record that they are often the most popular. But quite the worst are proletarian tragedies of an even more sentimental pseudo-realism. The author belabours some unsurprising social truth such as that ten people living in a small house are incommoded for lack of room, or that a fire starting in a coal pit is exceedingly dangerous for the miners who happen to be below. These plays would be slightly more bearable if the authors did not have such a portentous air of revelation. They belong to the same class of literature as *No Mean City*, and afford proof that back numbers of *Forward* or resurrected speeches by Keir Hardie do not form the best raw material for a play that people will willingly pay good money to see.

The liveliest and most genuinely native part of the Glasgow theatrical effort is played by the music-hall and pantomime comedians. Harry Lauder, like Burns, was of an East-Coast family, though bred in the West. He was the first man to make a world-wide reputation as a Scottish comedian. He set the fashion for dressing in the kilt and making frequent references to Highland heather and bluebells and Highland Jeanies and Marys. But neither his singing nor his speaking voice had the faintest trace of the Highland lilt. His speech was a full and satisfactory Braid Scots. When he began his career, some Scots were surprised and others were indignant at such a patently Lowland comedian dressing up as a Highlandman.

The surprise was unjustified, but the indignation was not. Lauder's kilt and curly walking stick were not a Highland disguise, but a Highland "take-off", a caricature. Whether he knew it or not, Lauder was following a long Lowland tradition in guying the Highlander. His stage get-up was conceived in the same spirit as the stage Irishman's clay pipe, shillelagh and battered caubeen. "The Bonnie Banks o' Clyde", not the Great Glen or Moray's silver sands, was the inspiration of Lauder's sometimes painful sentiment.

Lauder was not a comedian at all in the ordinary sense. He was an entertainer, or, as he said himself, a minstrel. His acting ability was very limited and his humour unremarkable, but he had an excellent voice and a truly commanding stage presence. As the theatrical public are always right, it must be conceded that he was a great performer, but as he grew older he went further away from the comic tradition which he never fully interpreted.

Will Fyfe was nearer to the real thing. He did not, in fact, belong to Glasgow, but to Dundee, yet he earned

Transatlantic popularity for a song which expressed the true Glasgow spirit in a heavily diluted but not in a falsified form. Dave Willis is nearer still. He was unfortunate in that his close resemblance to Hitler had to remain a frozen asset. Before the War, he was officially discouraged from making use of this happy endowment. When war broke out, there was no further official care for Hitler's feelings, but the Fuhrer had abruptly ceased to be a subject for mirth, even in caricature.

Lauder and Fyfe and Willis can all be reckoned as comedians who are, in varying degrees, the interpreters of an artificial dramatic convention. They may be counted as "Scotch" comedians, good in their kind, but the kind is not authentic. But the strictly Glasgow comedians are Glasgow from the toes up. Their humour and their type-impersonations are immediately recognizable by a Glasgow audience from the depths of their own experience. For that reason, they do not travel well, but this is no great hardship for them. Several Glasgow comics have made steady incomes that a West End star might envy, without ever going further south than Carlisle.

Tommy Lorne is still loved and lamented by a multitude. His long melancholy face, his sensitive hands and his air of timid and ingratiating bewilderment conveyed that air of pathos which is alleged to be the basis of the best comedy. But Tommy never sank into sentimentality. He disdained that mean pandering to easy emotionalism, considering that a comic turned tear-jerker was no better than a concert pianist who tried to hold his audience by doing conjuring tricks in the intervals of his playing.

After Lorne's untimely death, Tommy Morgan may be considered the most popular of the Glasgow School of

Comics. He is less subtle than Lorne was, less of a artist, but his broad appeal is emphatic and immensely popular. Like Lorne, Morgan is of Irish extraction. It may be significant that the two men who have broken most emphatically away from the Scotch comic's convention were not influenced by national ancestral memories of the pure Scot. They both might be said to belong to Glasgow more unconditionally than Will Fyfe ever could belong, even if he had been born and bred in the city.

Yet, it must be admitted that the Glasgow comic who is most completely liberated in soul is not a man of Irish extraction, but a woman of Scotch extraction. Doris Droy is the Queen of the Queen's, that small and profoundly proletarian music-hall behind Glasgow Cross. Her approach is direct and dynamic and her voice would make a pneumatic road drill or an electric riveting machine sound like the soft purring of a contented cat. If it may be said that Lorne and Morgan sprang directly from the Glasgow earth, then Doris has not even sprung. Her impersonations of a female red biddy drinker or an alcoholic office cleaner are as realistic as Theodore Dreiser, but considerably more entertaining. She is a completely authentic interpreter of Glasgow life on the basement level. It is weak to say that she belongs to Glasgow. Glasgow belongs to her.

There are other comics who may lack the rending quality of Doris Droy, who pierces both the heart and the ear, but still have genuine merit of a more modest kind. All come into their own in the pantomime season. Glasgow's passion for pantomime is even greater than its passion for musical comedy. Year after year, the Princess Theatre (now the Citizens') ran a pantomime which would brook no rivalry in the whole of Britain. Starting before Christmas, it would show no signs of flagging until Easter. Comics who first found fame in the Princess might graduate to more profitable theatres, but they never did better work, and they sometimes deteriorated. The Princess was not the essence of Glasgow comedy, for the fine distilled methylated spirit of Glasgow is to be found only in the Queen's, but it was as near to the real thing as the paying public would stand in large and economic numbers. There are wanton and deplorable lowbrows in Glasgow who wish well enough to the Citizens' Theatre, but still think it is a poor exchange for the Princess pantomime which it suppressed.

It may be objected that comics at pantomimes are hardly "culture" as the word is understood by the architects of the Third Programme, but they are "culture" in the wider and more tolerable sense. They come much nearer to the truth of the Gorbals than any dialectical exposure has ever done. Unity Theatre which is a Marxist rival of the Citizens may preen itself on its unflinching realism, but the slum-dwellers of Glasgow see more of themselves on the pantomime stage than they could in the Unity Theatre, to which as a matter of fact they never go. Unity is supported mostly by professional Communists and ideological school-teachers.

Some years ago, Glasgow earned a rather surprising reputation for verse speaking. This rather dreary occupation became popular under the inspiration of a memorable teacher and John Masefield, who adjudicated at a kind of verse-speaking Cup Final, said that Glasgow was a "nest of nightingales". This verdict was received in stunned silence.

The Musical Festival has always produced good choral singing, and the Orpheus Choir, now abruptly and unnecessarily defunct, had almost an international reputation. Its technical excellence was beyond dispute, but its repertoire was rather simple-minded and one-sided for

"MUSIC"

such unregenerate creatures as myself, who find that a little Hebridean folk-music goes a very long way.

Glasgow is not a conspicuously musical city, and is certainly not a nest of composers, though the songs of Scott have a more than local reputation. Still less is Glasgow a city of poets. A long, long time ago, Thomas

Campbell wrote several good poems, but since then nothing much has happened in the poetic lay. There was a poet called Alexander Smith whose name may still be found in the index of any really thorough history of nine-teenth-century literature, but the most loyal Glasgow man could not read Smith's verse and still maintain that it was much to be proud of.

The best of the local verse-writing is humorous. "Serious" verse-writing has not yet fully recovered from the Burns hang-over. For a century and a half, Robert Burns has afflicted Scottish verse like the potato blight. Burns himself was a highly literary gent, but his superb success encouraged long generations of poetasters to imagine that the most inept banalities and the grossest sentimentality could be passed for respectable verse when trimmed with a few lamentable remnants of "the Doric". There has been, in modern times, a breakaway from the bastard vocabulary and "sentiments" of the Burns tradition, but the most interesting and also the most eccen-tric of the younger and fresher poets come from the North and East of Scotland and not from Glasgow.

Prose is more in Glasgow's line, and factual prose at that, as may be seen from the Glasgow newspapers. The *Glasgow Herald* is, of course, the sage and reverend signor of the tribe. An uncle of mine read the *Herald* leaders every day for almost eighty years. It had a memorable effect upon his conversation. The *Herald* never quite reached to the international eminence achieved by the *Manchester Guardian* under the exces-sively lamented C. P. Scott, but its influence is more than local, and its standards are high. It has guided the Glasgow *bourgeoisie* firmly away from a vain Liberalism to a solid, middle-of-the-road Conservatism. If the *bourgeoisie* are not entirely sure what road they are in the middle of, the *Herald* can hardly be blamed for a dubiety which appears to be endemic to Conservatism all over the contemporary world.

With four morning and three evening newspapers, Glasgow is not short of something to read on the tram. Competition is lively and local news is heavily emphasized, particularly in the evening papers. There are journalists of high ability and some of scholarship, working in the Glasgow press, although the Scottish export of talent is heavier in journalism than in any other activity. It is a pity that a town with such a considerable educated element does not have a serious monthly magazine or even a "quality" Sunday newspaper. Support could surely be found among the public who eagerly bought the *Glasgow Evening News* when the late Neil Munro made that paper easily the liveliest and the most intelligent evening paper in Britain.

Glasgow's intellectual activity may be unpretentious and conducted without fuss, but it is still considerable. Serious-minded men and women suffer highbrow lectures with stubborn fortitude. The excellent bookshops are heavily patronized. The Scottish Orchestra commands respectable support and Glasgow people have been known to pay money to listen to Bach recitals.

All in all, Glasgow pursues Beauty and Truth without excitement, but at a sober and determined pace. And it must be suggested once again that the best conversation in Glasgow is better than the best anywhere else in the British Isles.

CHAPTER ELEVEN

FUN AND GAMES

A VISITOR to Glasgow who formed his impression of the people by looking at the faces in the street would not readily guess that they have an absorbing passion for dancing. But such is the case.

In all industrial cities, dancing is a highly popular amusement, but in Glasgow it is something more. It is almost a Way of Life. Perhaps dancing provides an outlet for a rumbustious and highly emotional people who chafe against inhibitions and conventions which they hardly know how to defy.

Whatever the explanation, the fact is undeniable. All kinds of dancing come alike to Glasgow. In the High-landers Institute can be heard the quick pattering of light feet in the reels and the loud and piercing yells that are a vital part of these exhausting exercises. The floors of small halls in back streets are apt to sag alarmingly when rather too many Irish dancers go through the movements of "The Waves of Tory". Old-fashioned dancing is immensely popular, nor are the modern modes despised. On the whole, preference is shown to the kinds of dancing which demand vigorous physical effort and a good deal of noise. They provide the best release for the struggling Glasgow spirit.

The big dance halls of the Palais type are much the same in Glasgow as elsewhere, but the bubbling, spontaneous dancing spirit is more fully expressed in small and shabby halls. The police do not regard these halls with undisguised favour. Often enough the management takes an elastic view of the permissible number, accommodation is primitive, and there is an occasional brawl when green-eyed jealousy takes possession of some cutthroat cavalier. Then there is a scurry of women to the door and a chorus of screams until the cavalier is thrown, not unprotesting, downstairs. When a number of cavaliers start trouble as a gang, they occasionally succeed in throwing the management downstairs.

The etiquette of a tough dance-hall is strict enough. Fiery spirits are quick to take offence. The "Excuse me" dance frequently leads to misunderstanding. A man of sensitive honour does not allow himself to be robbed of his partner after only a few steps. Eyes, and sometimes razors, flash defiance. Conciliatory words are uttered in vain. One thing leads to another, as the saying goes, and sometimes the other leads to a term in jail.

There is no dance-hall manager who would not thankfully bar the door to the tough characters, if they only knew how, but as often as not the responsible man is merely a hall caretaker of advanced years and enfeebled physique, who would be more suitably employed as a night watchman. In districts where resort to the police is regarded with indignant disfavour, there is not much the poor man can do but hope for the best, and keep out of the way when the worst comes.

Yet, "the jiggin' " loses none of its immense popularity. The girls who rend heaven with their frightened cries one night, are back the next night rending heaven with their yells of boisterous pleasure. Far from damping their zeal, the risk of a brawl adds an extra spice to an evening's amusement which is exhilarating enough even without a breach of the peace.

Violence, of course, is not the normal thing in the small and fusty dance-halls, but the vigour of the dance does sometimes stimulate the angry passions. On occasion it also stimulates the passion of love, and imported screw-tops, consumed in the dressing-room if there is one, do nothing to encourage moderation of feeling. Even in the most respectable evening dress affairs of the *bourgeoisie*, there is an undercurrent of excitement and potential abandon not to be met with in the dances of the more placid southern climes.

The most vigorous of the Dissenting Kirks still come down on dancing with the heaviest of hands, but their influence in Glasgow is negligible. Their monitory voice is drowned by the "Hoochs" of the dancers and the cry of the M.C., "swap partners and burl". There may be a trace of Puritan disapproval in the pedantic insistence by the local authorities that there should be some ready means of escape from a dance hall, that the elements of hygiene shall be provided, and that the floor should offer decent prospects of resisting the impact of an Eightsome Reel. But, although disapproval may make itself felt in indirect ways, dancing does not rouse crusading fervour in the way that gambling and drink and Sabbath-breaking do.

Though there is no organized body dedicated to the suppression of dancing, it is a curious fact that the Catholic Church, which is immensely more tolerant than the Established Kirk in other regards, looks on dancing without much favour. There is a suspicion of dancing as a fruitful occasion of goings-on, and there is also a solid local objection on the ground that dancing is one of the main causes of mixed marriages. There is a popular belief that the Catholic Church encourages mixed marriages as a useful means of securing converts, but nothing could be further from the truth. The rulers of the Church would rejoice if it were possible to prohibit mixed marriage altogether.

That, however, is not practical politics, but the Church does what it can to discourage them. The Church is well aware that not all the thunderbolts of the civil and ecclesiastical law would stop Glasgow folk from dancing, but attempts have been made to cater for this unconquerable urge, under proper safeguards, by permitting Catholic Parish dances to which only Catholics are, in theory, admitted. It is said that intending dancers have been asked, from time to time, to give proof of their Catholicity and that young men who entertain a devastating indifference to all religion have done some earnest homework with the Catholic girl friend to learn enough to scrape through an examination which must necessarily be something less than fundamental.

Although the Established Presbyterian Kirk has no positive, or even negative, attitude towards dancing, the Sabbath cuts across the dancing week like the voice of a peremptory M.C. calling for a halt. All Saturday dances end on or before midnight, and on Sunday the lightest and most lissome folk must keep their feet still and ease their souls with what refreshment they can find in the *News of the World*. The voice of an ancient past commands rest upon that day, and Glasgow obeys.

Dancing is a liberation passionately valued which Puritanism hesitates to condemn outright. Once a year, there is liberation on a much wider scale with no regard at all for the frown of the Kirk. Hogmanay, the last day of the year, is the day when almost anything goes. By tradition and by principle, the Presbyterian Kirk comes down heavily on any suggestion of respect for the Calendar of Saints. It is perhaps not surprising that the people should respond by celebrating the Calendar itself. But, just as children in other countries get a greater thrill and a deeper excitement out of Christmas Eve than out of Christmas Day, so do Glasgow men enjoy the eve of New Year more than Ne'erday itself.

All the innate sentimentality of the Scot oozes out in a rich and treacly flood as the last hours of the last day of the year wear on. Hard-bitten riveters and hard-boiled business men wait with glistening eyes for the peal of midnight. When the last stroke spells the death of the old year, they gulp heavily for one or both of two obvious reasons and shake hands all round with a solemn fervour that can only be described as religious.

But sentimentality is soon swamped by utterly unrestricted hilarity. All normal restraints are flung aside, as the first-footers set out, footloose and carefree, armed with a lump of coal, a piece of bun and a bottle of cordial liquor. For that night the cause of temperance goes down in total rout. Men who normally take care never to be seen in a pub pass the bottle openly round in the street and in all-night trams and buses. All through the night, Glasgow is as lively as an anthill. A large number of Glasgow men would consider it irreverent to go to bed at all on Hogmanay, and lights blaze in nearly every window till dawn. Hogmanay is a completely whole-hearted spree on a lavishly royal scale.

At one time, the focal point of rejoicing was Glasgow Cross. There thousands gathered to indulge in hoarse and hearty song, and to fling their empty bottles with a satisfying smash against the statue of King Billy. There was no historical or ideological judgment implied in the bottle-throwing. Bottles were heaved by Orangemen who regarded the Boyne as a prouder victory than Blenheim, Trafalgar and Waterloo all rolled into one. They threw their bottles at King Billy because he happened to be there.

This custom was abruptly ended when the statue was removed to an inconspicuous site in Cathedral Square. The removal was explained on grounds of traffic convenience, but there were dark suspicions that the sourpuss element in the Corporation seized the traffic excuse to put an end to a piece of healthy and invigorating fun.

However, the festival has been more seriously affected by the scarcity and the high price of whisky in post-war years. A Glasgow man will go to great lengths to get hold of a bottle of whisky for Hogmanay. Other drinks may do more or less well for other occasions, but only whisky can bring in the New Year in a decent and traditional manner. Publicans are harassed on all hands, and are forced to hoard their stores. They are pestered out of their wits as much by their friends as by their customers. In the days of most acute scarcity, some publicans opened a register of demands five or six weeks in advance of the sacred day. The regular customer who failed to apply in time had only himself to blame, but that did not prevent him from blaming the publican.

New Year's Day is Hangover Day. A stranger who has joined in the previous night's fun and looks for a hair of the dog will find that all the kennels are closed. Every single pub is shut, but all prudent Glasgow men keep something hidden away to see them through the long dry day.

There is much family visiting on Ne'erday. Shortbread and the staggeringly indigestible black-bun are forced on every visitor with, of course, a drop of something. For several days there is much party-giving and visiting, but nothing to resemble the one wild night of Hogmanay. The Beltane fires of the rebellious Glasgow spirit are damped down under the "blue, bleak embers" of the serious working year. "Back to parritch and auld claes" is the command of economic necessity and stern convention. Glasgow has had its one completely unbridled annual fling.

The nearest approach is the Burns Supper season. Round about the twenty-fifth of January, the faithful assemble to honour the Immortal Memory.

A Burns Supper has to be seen to be believed. It is a ritualistic occasion. There is the piping in of the haggis, the whisky for the piper, the recitation of the Burns Grace and the great oration. Immortal Memory speeches resemble nothing so much as the conventional orations which are mouthed at the funeral of a barbaric chief. There is the same floridity of language, the same hyperbole of praise and the same enormity of claim.

But the parallel is by no means complete, for, as likely as not, the Burns orator believes every word he utters. He believes that Rabbie starts off the same mark as Shakespeare in the poetic sprint. He believes also that in philosophic insight, Rabbie yields nothing to Immanuel Kant, that his social witness is the brightest light a dark, distracted world has ever seen, and that the tender and noble qualities of his character should be an example to us all.

When it comes to character, the orator must check

"IMMORTAL MEMORY"

for a moment in the high flight of his eloquence to refer to the undeniable fact that the master of song was also not quite indifferent to the charms of wine and women. But a really practised orator has little difficulty in turning Rabbie's little failings to his advantage. Who taught the world to be gentle with human weaknesses? Why, none other than Rabbie himself, and the world is bound in decency to be gentle with him. His faults make him all the more endearing. The listeners who hear this sales-talk every year nod in solemn approval of the originality and profundity of the observations.

Platitudes and clichés pour out from the orator in an endless flow. Thirty years ago, it was frequently claimed that Rabbie was the spiritual father of the League of Nations. He is still described as the spiritual father of Socialism and as a patriot of equal stature with William Wallace. Occasionally some clerical orator will venture to suggest that he was fundamentally in moral and mental agreement with John Knox, but this suggestion is not well received. Rabbie is loved as the man who cocked a snook at the heirs of John Knox, but who could also write sen-timentally about the old ha' Bible and family prayers.

Once the Immortal Memory has been celebrated with a due mixture of hilarity and solemnity, there are no set occasions for general frolics till summer. Of course, there are jolly weddings, and even jollier funerals and other private occasions for mirth. but the town recognizes no public feasts. Easter means little, except a long week-end, and Whitsun means even less.

But July brings Glasgow Fair, and an outrush to the sea. A large majority of working-class holiday-makers seldom go further away than the Clyde coast. The holiday resorts have to some extent suburbanized the beautiful Clyde estuary, They have a Victorian flavour and offer nothing resembling the elaborate artificial attractions of Brighton, Blackpool or Southend. The piers are stout affairs with a strictly practical purpose and built to withstand the heavy battering of the winter storms. There are no pier concert halls or toy railways, and, as far as the Clyde is concerned, the butler never saw anything.

There are highly genteel resorts, such as Troon, where the *bourgeoisie* spend a leisurely holiday. The brief carnival of the Fair means little to them, and they would love to think it meant nothing. The fine frenzy of the Fair season is to be found in the popular places, like Gourock, Rothesay and Dunoon. During the Fair fortnight, Montague Street (robustly mispronounced) in Rothesay is remarkably like the Gallowgate of Glasgow.

In the cheaper streets of the cheaper resorts, there is heavy overcrowding and some degree of overcharging. Clydeside landladies have always charged remarkably high for the quality of lodgings they can offer. Even in those lodgings which are some degrees better than mere bunk accommodation, the aspidistra still stands in the window-sill and anyone studying the pictures and the furniture might be excused for beginning to feel anxious about the dangerous position of poor General Gordon.

Big Dippers and Towers and fancy piers would be no welcome addition to the Firth of Clyde, but better lodgings certainly would. When the weather is good, a Clydeside holiday is an open-air holiday. The hardy men of the yards toil enthusiastically at the oars of sturdy rowing boats. Not for them the effeminate luxury of cushions, and the ignominy of being rowed by a boatman. Even in summer, the Clyde can be rough and rowing is challengingly hard work. Yachting can be even harder. The hills come down so sharply to the water's edge that sudden and dangerous gusts are common enough. Anyone who is liable to turn seasick or objects to getting soaked had better not try yachting on the Clyde.

Unfortunately, there is an equal danger of being soaked on land. The West of Scotland is rainy for most of the year, and July is one of the rainiest months. There are few more depressing spectacles than the promenade of Rothesay or Dunoon on a thoroughly bad day during the Fair. A cold and high wind throws rain by the handful into the faces of the small number of dour and spirited men who trudge along with their heads down, determined to enjoy themselves, even if it kills them. The shelters are packed with bleak-faced women and disconsolate children.

It sometimes happens that all the days of the Fair are bad. When that happens, the working-class mother in cramped and dingy lodgings finds her holiday a nightmare. Outside rain pours down with unrelenting persistence, and inside the air is damp with the stale steam from drying clothes. The rowing boats are all turned turtle on the shore, there are huddled queues outside the shops and there is a rush for the pubs and the pictures in the evening.

It is in a thoroughly bad season of weather that the poor quality of Clydeside lodgings is exposed. When rowing and walking, golf and sea-bathing are impossible, the holiday-makers would be more comfortable if they were home in Govan or Bridgeton.

But, no matter how loud and deep the victims may curse when the sky opens on them, the Fair remains fixed to the middle of July, and the victims cling stubbornly in their favourite resorts. There are some who swear by Arran, where even the rain is of superior quality, and others who would feel that anarchy had entered their lives if they went anywhere else than Rothesay or Dunoon.

This conservatism is highly agreeable to the landladies and shopkeepers and the local authorities of the Clyde, but there would be a sharp improvement of holiday conditions if the chill wind of competition blew down some of the promenades. There is no suggestion that the Clyde should be further vulgarized, for there is rather too much of half-hearted and pathetic vulgarity already. But something should be done to raise the level of ordinary comfort. The little seaside towns are pleasant enough to look at in an old-fashioned way. The scenery is superb and there is everything that could be asked for in an active open-air holiday provided only that the weather is good. But the weather is often bad, and it is not too much to ask that the people who make their living out of Glasgow should provide Glasgow with somewhere decent to get in out of the rain.

However, when the sun is shining, the Clyde is a most admirable holiday area. The estuary itself is an endless entertainment for people who know about ships. Knowing men and even more knowing boys study the ship traffic with a profoundly expert eye. As a number of the holiday resorts can be reached from Glasgow only by sea, the estuary is brisk with excellent and most cheerful-looking passenger steamers. They looked even more cheerful in the days when the rival railway companies had their own funnel colours and sometimes raced each other for the piers. There was passionate partisanship among small boys, and for some mysterious reason the *Caley* commanded the widest and most romantic allegiance. At the time of the great railway mergers, the Scottish railway lines lost their identity and now the drab mantle of nationalisation covers all. Colour has gone out of the Clyde scene.

The great yachting event, the Clyde Fortnight, is also something less than it was. There are still exciting races with much skilful sailing, but the really big yachts, like heavyweight boxers, have a special appeal of their own. However, a big yacht demands a big fortune, and the great races which roused such lively interest thirty years ago are now only a fading memory, with *Shamrock*, *White Heather* and the rest.

This was only to be expected in such a dismally egalitarian age, but the noble estuary still offers a great variety of natural attractions with all the possibilities of a healthy and invigorating holiday, so long as the rain keeps off. But Glasgow people are not easily downed by the weather either on holiday or at home. On the coldest and darkest night, a big fight will attract a huge crowd, to stand in the open air and cheer madly for their man.

Until the end of the first World War, there was no great enthusiasm for boxing in Glasgow, for the good enough reason that there was nothing much to be enthusiastic about.

Then, suddenly, Glasgow began to produce excellent boxers at the lighter weights, particularly the fly weight. The greatest of these was undoubtedly Benjamin Lynch. There are sound judges who consider him to have been the greatest flyweight of all time, but he became a local legend at least as much for the oddities of his character as for his proficiency in the ring.

"Wee Benny" was to Scottish boxing what Terry

McGovern was to America and Young Griffo to Australia. He looked upon the wine when it was red or any other colour, and his faithful followers were continually disturbed by rumours that he would soon be confined in the cooler.

In his prime he had a rosy, clear complexion that was an eminently misleading testimonial to a clean and careful life. When he was in reasonably good condition, he could beat any rival without much difficulty, but he was sometimes in unreasonably bad condition. To put it mildly he was eccentric. It is said that he once punched a horse on the nose because it was laughing at him. In jovial mood, he would take a taxi from pub to pub standing drinks all round until, in the pregnant local phrase, "he couldnae bite his finger".

Although he left almost everything to be desired in the way of civic and personal propriety, he was a model of decorum and chivalry in the ring. He lost his world title in a manner that must be without precedent in boxing history. He lost it, before the fight, on the scales. That was bad enough. But Benny did not merely fail to make the flyweight limit of eight stone. He also failed to make the bantam weight limit of eight stone six. When his weight was announced in a rather strangled voice as eight stone seven and a half pounds, the presiding officer announced that Lynch would have until four o'clock to take off the extra beef. As nothing short of an amputation would do the trick, the announcement was an empty formality, but Benny made a highly painful occasion even worse than it need have been. He stepped nimbly from the scales and cheerfully said, "Now for a bloody good feed".

His American challenger misguidedly agreed to meet him at catch weights. The huge crowd angrily booed Benny when he stepped into the ring, but the champion who had thrown his crown away was entirely unperturbed, and he trounced the American with such emphasis and ease that he left the ring to a storm of cheers. He fought a few times after this triumph, but with declining success and with hardly a pretence of training. In his last fight, happily not in Glasgow, he fell down when his opponent hit him, and fell down again when he hit his opponent. This was plainly not a satisfactory method of conducting a boxing contest, and Benny's services were no longer anywhere required. Yet, in spite of his total collapse, there was no resentment against poor Benny. Rather, there was a secret chuckling appreciation of a man who could be so serenely indifferent to the formidable social sanctions of Glasgow town. His end came suddenly. He walked into an infirmary one day, complaining that he felt unwell. Soon after he was dead. He left a fortune of seven or eight pounds.

Lynch was not the only top-flight Glasgow boxer. Jackie Paterson recaptured the flyweight championship for the city, and several others have been good enough to fight for the world's title at their own weight, though not quite good enough to win. There is a steady and sufficient support for amateur boxing and for the more modest professional fights, but the huge crowds for the infrequent big fights are mostly drawn from people whose interest in boxing is fitful and whose enthusiasm is stirred only by a clash of celebrities.

It is not so with football, which is a steady and absorbing interest. Rugby is played by all of the middle-class schools. The keenest local rivalry is between the High School and the Academy. Both the present and the former pupils of these schools battle against each other with much zeal and spirit. The conflict of the Academy and High School F.P.'s and the Inter-City with Edinburgh are the highlights of the Glasgow Rugby Year, but although the Rugby addicts are profoundly interested, a great majority of the population do not even know when these matches are being played.

Association football is the overwhelming sporting interest of Glasgow. It is sometimes said by the more foolish or perhaps by the more snobbish Rugby enthusiasts that the great Soccer crowds are mere masses of spectators watching paid performers but taking no part in the game themselves. This is a false and shallow judgment. The local passion is as much for playing football as for watching it. There are schoolboys who get up at five of a summer's morning to get in an hour of football before they set off on their milk or newspaper rounds. The football pitches provided by the schools and the Corporation are quite insufficient to meet the immense demand. Every piece of waste ground is utilized, legally or illegally. A rubber ball or even a rolled-up piece of paper will do for a scratch game, with jackets for goal-posts and perhaps a police-watcher instead of a referee.

If the majority of the spectators at the big matches do not play football regularly or in regular teams, neither do the majority of Rugby supporters. Football under either code is a young man's game, but men who could not possibly last a full soccer game on a full-sized pitch snatch every chance to kick a ball around. The great crowds for the great matches are composed of men who know the game intimately because they played it hard and often so long as they were able. They make immense noise and their arguments are passionate and profane, but it is the violence of experts. They know what they are talking about, and they never indulge in the merely ignorant clamour of a big boxing crowd.

The greatest occasion of the Soccer year is the International against England. When the match is played at Wembley, thousands take the train from Glasgow, armed with bottles and decorated with tartan scarves and tammies. They show perhaps rather too much of the Hogmanay spirit. The Londoners enjoy the colour, the pranks and the cheerful shouting, but they are hardly to be blamed if they are confirmed in their suspicion that a good many people in Glasgow drink a great deal too much. The invading Scots make a kind of proletarian Boat Race night out of the Wembley International. In essentials they may behave better than the Boat Race crowds but they certainly show the Londoners a more virile and violent conception of a good time than they are accustomed to. After the last international, I came back from Wembley by train. There was a Glasgow man keeping himself upright with much difficulty in the middle of the crowded compartment. It could justly be said that he was dressed for the part. In addition to the obligatory tartan scarf and tammy, he was wearing a kilt, with a whitewash brush for sporran and a dustbin lid (City of Westminster) for a Highland targe. "I'll no' be worth tuppence the nicht," he said, with a beaming and confiding air. "Tae tell you the truth, I'm no' worth fourpence the noo." But, although the shades of mental night were closing in on him, he argued aggressively and persistently, with nobody replying, that the English had been supremely lucky to lose by only one goal, and that the Scottish eleven was individually superior in every position and even more heavily superior as a team.

His combative spirit was characteristic. The Glasgow man does not go to an International with any intention of distributing polite and impartial approval to both sides. He goes with the sole purpose of yelling himself into a frenzy in support of Scotland. The most brilliant demonstration of football skill gives him no satisfaction at all if Scotland fails to win.

His partisan passion is shown even more clearly when the match is played at Hampden Park, Glasgow. It has been said that the "Hampden Roar" is worth a goal to the Scottish team. This is very likely untrue, but the Roar is nevertheless an intimidating and electrifying affair. There may have been something like it at the Fall of the Bastille, but there is nothing like it in any other sporting event in Britain. There is no malice behind the Roar, but only an ungovernable excitement and an intolerable anxiety that Scotland should win.

And yet, although the International draws the biggest crowd, it is not the most intense occasion of the football year. The clashes between Celtic and Rangers, the two leading Glasgow teams, rouse deeper and more dramatic passions, for these matches crystallize the racial and religious difficulties of Glasgow. The Battle of the Boyne, the Reformation, Irish Partition and all kinds of local rows and ructions play their part in inflaming feeling.

Celtic are identified with the Catholic interest and

Rangers with the Orange. It makes no difference that some of the greatest Celtic heroes have been Protestants.* These men are accepted as honorary Catholics, for football purposes, just as Mr. Attlee and Mr. Gaitskell are accepted as honorary toilers for political purposes. The identification may be arbitrary, but it is quite good enough for the faithful followers.

For many happy years, a Celtic versus Rangers match gave the highest degree of pleasurable excitement to everybody except the police. The shock troops on either side were organized in brake-clubs. A brake-club was a kind of Unfriendly Society of men who travelled to the match in their own hired bus. They wore tin helmets, club scarves and tammies and rosettes and carried ricketties and banners and bugles, and sometimes a useful supply of rivets or pieces of paving-stone. Frequently battles broke out while the brake-clubs were converging on the football ground, until the police laid it down that the Celtic clubs must approach the ground from one end and the Rangers' clubs from the other. Next, the banners and the ricketties were forbidden, and all practical steps have been taken to put an end to fighting and stone and bottle throwing.

In days when feeling ran even higher than now, the frenzy of the supporters found a readier echo on the field. Play was frequently described as "robust", which meant that a fair shoulder charge began with the heel of the boot

---

* One Protestant Celtic player was transferred to an English team. When he came back to Glasgow he complained to his close friend, a Catholic Celt, that an English player had called him a Papist bastard.

The Catholic Celt laughed indulgently.

"They call me that every Saturday," he said.

"But that's different," said the Protestant ex-Celt with simple earnestness, "you are one."

and ended with the back of the head. Every foul or alleged foul brought forth a cry of execration,

> "as if men fought upon the earth
> And fiends in upper air."

A bad (or inconveniently good) decision by the referee brought a volley of outraged abuse and sometimes a volley of stones as well. A goal for one side or the other was greeted by a triumphant bawling of "Boyne Water" or "Hail Glorious Saint Patrick". Such an atmosphere could not fail to have its effect on the players, already excited by an exhausting and doubtful struggle. It is said that during one particularly ferocious game, the Celtic captain was exasperated when play was halted because of damage to the ball. "Never mind the ba'," he is alleged to have shouted, "get on wi' the gemme." No doubt the story is an invention, but it has symbolic value, and it is significant that the Celtic captain was a Protestant.

The temperature of those invigorating contests is not quite so high as it used to be, which is a loss to sporting excitement but a gain to public order. Yet it remains true that the diehard supporter of each side every Saturday gives his zealous support to his own team and support no less zealous to the team which happens to be playing the enemy. If the crowd at Celtic Park hear that Rangers have gone down before Hearts or Dundee, they raise three hearty though not particularly British cheers. Equally, Rangers supporters take vast pleasure in the defeat of Celtic. Yet, on one occasion, there was something like unanimity. That was on the dramatic day when Rangers played Moscow Dynamo. The Dynamo were a Communist team, and they were also a police team. The most fiery Celtic supporters agreed that for this one day, they must wish well of Rangers. It took an immense moral effort to decide that there was something in the world more important than the local football feud, but the decision was made. All honour to these worthy men.

The players of the two teams are friendly off the field and in modern times they do not start a match with any prior intention of kicking each other around. There are still outbursts of violence on and off the field, but sometimes the teams will play each other for several games running with perfect sportsmanship and propriety.

And yet, the atmosphere of a Celtic-Rangers match is like no other. Stricter control and perhaps some softening of feeling have done a good deal to mitigate the violence, but the Celtic versus Rangers contest is still the most obvious indication of the social, racial and religious frictions and unresolved stresses of a city which has still something to learn in the way of tolerance. The contest takes the lid off The Problem.

CHAPTER TWELVE

THE PROBLEM

IF the strength of a Church is measured by the numbers who accept its doctrines and its discipline, then the Catholic Church is without doubt the largest and most important Church in Glasgow. It lacks the official prestige of the Established Kirk and the social prestige of the Episcopalian, but it commands the allegiance of its members to an extent which all the other Churches might, and do, envy. In some Catholic parishes there is standing room only, every Sunday of the year, at the more convenient Masses. In heavily industrial parishes the first Mass of the Sunday may begin before six in the morning, and the same is true of the occasional great Feast Days, when Mass attendance is binding, although the Feast falls on a working day. A quite sizeable minority of Catholics attend Mass every day of the year.

This does not mean that one hundred per cent of the nominal Catholics of Glasgow are one hundred per cent devout. There are many indifferent, irregular and even lapsed Catholics particularly in the slum districts, but the average "careless" Catholic attends his church more frequently than the average Protestant Church member who is regarded as being a solid supporter of his Church.

Any Catholic of the middle class who ceases to attend Mass regularly at once becomes the subject of gossip and conjecture, just as much as if he had publicly taken a mistress, and much more so than if he had gone heavily on the bottle. The higher in the economic or intellectual level, the more complete is the allegiance to the Faith. It would be safe to say that ninety-five per cent of the Catholic students of the University attend Sunday Mass with absolutely unfailing punctuality, even in circumstances of great difficulty. It would be unsafe to say that even ten per cent of the nominally Protestant students are to be found at Church every Sunday.

The contrast is sometimes explained away by the fact that Catholics are bound to go to Mass on Sunday. That is undoubtedly true, but John Knox would have bawled the roof off if anyone had dared to suggest that Presbyterians were not equally bound. Indeed a century and a half ago, a Presbyterian who was found in the streets when he should have been at Kirk ran some danger of being arrested. The moral and social compulsions have lapsed only because the great majority of non-Catholic Glasgow citizens have long ago gone on strike against them. It is significant that whereas the most rigid of the Sabbatarian propagandists are ready to assert that it is a sin to play tennis on Sunday, they seldom or never assert that it is a sin to give the Kirk a miss. The Protestant who attends his Kirk once a month is regarded as doing pretty well. The Catholic who fails to attend Mass once a week is regarded as putting his soul in dire and imminent peril.

The immense superiority of Catholic loyalty in religious observance is the first indisputable fact of The Problem. It is not a fact over which Catholics have any reason to crow, and the more intelligent Catholics are well aware of it. A Catholic minority can live more securely in a city of staunch though bigoted Protestants than in a city of greater tolerance but of rapidly spreading unbelief. When in 1918, the Catholic schools were taken into the public system, it became necessary to send a number of non-Catholic teachers of specialist subjects to Catholic schools. Some of the education officials thought it would be tactful to send teachers who had refused to take the Protestant training course in religious teaching, believing that they would be less hostile or prejudiced than those who were signed on for the other team. But the Catholic authorities would have none of them. If it was not yet possible to staff the Catholic schools with believing Catholics, then the deficiency must be made up by believing Protestants, but on no account by unbelievers.

This was an entirely logical attitude for a strictly doctrinal Church, but the possession of a Protestant religious certificate was no guarantee of acceptance of the fullness of any Protestant faith. Indeed, the contrast between Catholic and Protestant Glasgow in religious observance is less striking than the contrast in religious belief.

The difference is indicated clearly enough in that entertaining and instructive book, *The Scottish Churches' Handbook*. The statement of claim by the Established Church of Scotland takes three closely printed pages, but doctrine is disposed of in six lines, four of these lines being no more than a reference to the Westminster Confession of Faith (as modified by the several Declaratory Acts). All the rest of the statement is taken up by explanations of organization. The totally ignorant inquirer would learn, as to doctrine, only that "two Sacraments are observed". There is not even a forthright assertion that only two Sacraments should be observed. The thunder of Knox sounds very distant and far away.

The Scottish Episcopal Church is no more forthcoming. The doctrinal standpoint is, generally speaking, that of the three great Catholic creeds. The rest of the statement deals with organization and social work. "As modified," "generally speaking". This is not much like Sinai. It sounds as if the Tables of the Law are open to sub-editing.

The Catholic Church takes sixty-five lines to state its doctrinal position. "The doctrinal position is clear and distinctive. The final authority in all matters of faith, order and conduct is the Church, which cannot err in her teaching concerning faith and morals. The visible head of the Church is the Pope, who is infallible". "Generally speaking"—"as modified," versus "the Pope who is infallible".

There is the great gulf between the Catholic and the Protestant Churches. It is a gulf which sometimes depresses and sometimes irritates Protestants who are friendly disposed towards Catholics. These Protestants are willing to accept the ministrations of an Established cleric, a United Free, a Free, a Free Presbyterian, a Reformed Presbyterian, an Original Secession, an Episcopalian or a Reformed Episcopalian in the amiable cause of unity, and they are vexed or annoyed when they are so often reminded that the Catholics won't play. It would be well if they recognized, however sadly, that the Catholics will never play. The Catholic Church has taken up a position which cannot be abandoned without self-destruction.

It would be well also if non-Catholics who are interested

in religious tolerance would make some effort to discover
what the Catholic Church really teaches (and Catholics
might do some homework on the other side). The ignorance of Catholic teaching and practice by educated non-
Catholics is startling. Every fourth man they pass in
the street is a Catholic and yet they could not give the
most elementary summary of what that man believes.
If the gulf of doctrine is unbridgeable, there is no reason
why the gulf of incomprehension should not be filled up.
Ignorance on the Catholic side is equally great. Many
Protestants who admire the Catholic Church in its
historic and international position yet have a subconscious
feeling that the local branch is a rather superstitious
community of the ignorant and the poor whose social
behaviour is no brilliant testimonial to the edifying effects
of their religious observance. Many Catholics are happy
not to know what their Protestant friends believe, because
they suspect that those friends don't know themselves.

This is all a pity, for people who have to live together
can live more comfortably and more tolerantly if each
knows, at least roughly, what the other is looking for in
this life and the next. But if ignorance were really bliss,
then the religious life of Glasgow would be a jolly affair
indeed.

Whatever may be said in criticism of the Catholics of
Glasgow, it cannot be justly denied that they have made
considerable sacrifices for their religion. This is a fact
which should make more impression than it does on
Glasgow Presbyterians, who have their own fine tradition
of sacrifice.

In the closing years of the eighteenth century, a gossipy

inquirer who wrote under the name of Senex estimated that the Catholic population of Glasgow was thirty-nine. There were forty-three anti-Catholic societies, so it might be said that the Catholics were receiving individual attention though not of a benevolent kind. The numbers of Catholics rose in the early part of the nineteenth century with dizzy speed, but entirely by immigration. The Church authorities were well aware of the alien flavour of Glasgow Catholicity, and they tried to disguise it by making important appointments a preserve of a handful of Highland clergy. The policy was judicious, but it was carried so far that it provoked resentment among the immigrants, who began to feel that they were being treated as proletarians within the Church as well as in industry.

Catholic expansion was regarded with a good deal of suspicion, which was sometimes expressed by the hurling of insults and sometimes by the hurling of bricks. When the cultivated and amiable Sir James Mackintosh was Lord Rector of the University, he made a reference in his Rectorial Address to the building of the Catholic pro-Cathedral on Clydeside. He expressed genial gratification that such a thing should be possible, for it was a sign of a most welcome growth of religious tolerance. At this point in his Address the students kicked up such a violent and indignant shindy that Sir James was compelled to do some hasty ad-libbing and explain that nobody had a greater detestation than himself for Romish superstitions. Tolerance may have been growing, but it was not a very big boy yet.

In spite of their poverty and in spite of public disapproval, Catholics stuck faithfully to the task of building churches. Their effort was impressive, and to the burden of church building they added the burden of school building. Any poor Catholic parent who wanted schooling for his children could get it easily enough in a Protestant public school, but Catholics struggled hard to build a school in every parish. It was necessary to draw heavily on nuns and priests and brothers to staff the schools, but the majority of teachers were lay men and women who taught for wretchedly low salaries and had few chances of promotion. Many of these teachers were insufficiently trained, when they were trained at all, but for long generations they followed a devoted and sacrificial career.

Although the Catholic Church settled and established itself in Glasgow and was formidable in numbers before the middle of the nineteenth century, the alien flavour remained. As the total numbers grew, the proportion of Highland Catholics correspondingly shrank, and an Irish accent was heard in nearly every pulpit. Resentment against the Highland monopoly of the higher posts found increasing justification, but the Irish did not always allow for the substantial arguments that the Highlanders could advance.

The Irish priests were indispensable, and they were equally zealous and courageous—but they were Irish. A Highland bishop had the thistle and the rose carved on the baptismal font in the pro-Cathedral of Glasgow, but not the shamrock. That was not a good idea. The land of the shamrock was the land where most of the congregation and most of the money came from. But neither was it a good idea of the Irish priests to make Saint Patrick's Day a feast almost equal to Christmas and

Easter, while paying only the most formal respect to Saint Andrew's Day.

The small Catholic areas of the Highlands and Islands were, and still are, astonishingly fertile in priests, and the lay-folk were, and still are, of the most exemplary piety and generosity in support of the Church. In a country where Catholicism had been almost obliterated, they were the one proof of continuity, the one solid link with the pre-Reformation past. The Highlanders wanted to see again a truly national Catholic Church, and they knew that the Church would never be fully established and fully recognized until it became fully Scottish.

The Highlanders were right though not always wise in the way they went about things. They welcomed the Irish influx and clearly understood that it was only by Irish members that they could hope to build a strong and influential Church. But at times they looked like an impoverished country gentleman who has inherited a fortune from a chain of fish and chip shops. The money is thankfully received and is used to improve a run-down estate, but the gentleman fervently wishes that it had come from some other source, and is anxious not to identify himself with the vulgar trade which provides the cash.

The friction and cleavage within the Church were largely unknown to the outside world. Sometimes the outside world looked on the Church with hostility, sometimes with alarm, but seldom with intelligent interest. Catholics were multiplying with disturbing speed, but they were still alien in their ways, in their thoughts and even in their speech; they were in Glasgow, but not of it.

There were prominent men in Glasgow (including ministers) who were familiar with the ritual of the Mass through frequent attendance in Continental churches, but had never taken the trouble to look inside a Glasgow Catholic church. There were others who "knew everybody", that is, everybody of any account, in Glasgow, but who had never exchanged a word with a priest in their lives.

It must not be thought that the fault was entirely on one side. Glasgow Catholics of Irish extraction met suspicion with resentment. They claimed full citizen status without admitting the implications of that status. Sentimental palaver about the ould bog road and dear ould Donegal was something that the Scots could well understand, being expert themselves in the exile humbug. But Irish sentiment went much deeper than that. Feeling that they were not accepted as first-class citizens, they tended to withdraw inside themselves, and to look for slights in all directions.

The resentment of the Catholic community is not mere huffiness. There is a widespread belief among Catholics that their advance in the world is retarded by prejudice. With a minority this belief reaches a pitch of absurdity. A Catholic student has been known to explain his examination failure by bigotry or "the grip", when it was more easily explained by the fact that he scored ten per cent. A teacher who spent much time in organizing schools football had the right of seniority to the next vacancy on the Football Committee. Before the meeting he announced to all and sundry that, of course, he would not be chosen. After the meeting when he had been chosen automatically and without question, he muttered darkly about the cunning of the Protestants who did not expose themselves by turning him down.

The allegation of bigotry is a good cover for inefficiency and laziness, and is also a comforting indulgence of that self-pity to which the Celtic nature is sometimes inclined. But there is bigotry, in fact, much less than there used to be, not so much as Catholics are tempted to imagine, but, perhaps, more than well-meaning Protestants are willing to admit. The meteoric rise of the Scottish Protestant League is sufficient proof of the fact.

The extent of the bigotry is impossible to establish. It is noisy in the slums where the Celtic-Rangers conflict is the height of religious dispute. (It is unfortunate that marriages of mixed race and religion are most common in those areas where religious passions are most raw and unreasonable.) There is a residuum of quieter and meaner bigotry among some sections of the *bourgeoisie* and there is, of course, the hearty hostility of the large Orange population.

But the practical test is discrimination in employment. When an employer asks an applicant the name of his or her school, he may be seeking to bar Catholics by a shoddy and roundabout method, but he may not. One young Catholic boy accused a business man of using the school approach to find out his religion. The business man nearly climbed over the desk at him. He wanted to know the name of the boy's school because he wanted to know what training he had had, and he scored a clinching dialectical triumph by giving the boy the job.

Anxiety to keep Catholics out of a job is less important than determination to get somebody else in. The helpful shove, the quiet wangle and the backstairs bargain are practised with the greatest enthusiasm, and expertise. The most instructive and moving hour I ever spent in my life was in the company of two Glasgow men of large influence. They were in a mood of easy reminiscence, fighting their old battles over again. They recalled how they had secured an important post for one young man because the young man's auntie had sold sweets to the two worthy gentlemen when they were boys. Another man had been delicately eased out of a highly embarrassing predicament because he was the cousin of a man of standing who did not wish to be embarrassed even by proxy. Over a third case they sadly confessed defeat. This was an amiable youth who also had an aunt in a key position. They were on the very point of securing for him a comfortable salary, needless to say at the public expense, when he was abruptly sequestered from the public gaze owing to a combination of alcoholism and rapidly developing insanity.

All over Glasgow there are public-spirited men who spend a large part of their time making sure that no job worth having escapes from their relatives or their friends. As a consequence, the applicant who does not have an aunt who sold sweets to the right schoolboys is at a weighty disadvantage. As the Catholic community is ill-provided with influential aunts, a disappointed Catholic candidate is tempted to blame his disappointment on a positive hostility to himself or, rather, to his religion, whereas the real explanation is an amiable desire to do some service to the nephew of the woman who used to live next door to a man who has wires to pull.

In a number of careers a Catholic with qualifications equal to the other candidates for appointments or promotion is likely to come off worst. This is irritating to the man who is turned down, but it is no matter for surprise. The remedy is for Catholics to have better qualifications, or else to build up their own racket and acquire an armamentarium of plausible and persuasive aunts.

This can be done only if Catholics, however Irish their names may be, identify themselves wholeheartedly and unconditionally with the place where they live and mean to go on living. The born Irish are now a small minority of the Catholic population, and it is doubtful if even half of the Glasgow Catholics are entirely Irish even by remote extraction. There is no reason why an "Irishman" of the third or fourth generation should fear to speak of " 'Ninety-Eight," but it would be a relief if he spoke of something else.

Assimilation has proceeded far more rapidly and far more extensively than is generally realized. The children in Catholic schools for the most part regard themselves quite unself consciously as Scottish, and that is what they are. The barriers are breaking down in all directions. Glasgow has had to digest a very large immigrant meal, and the process was not assisted by the activities of the Loyal Orange Order. A difference that was racial, religious and social was not easily solved, and it cannot be said that either side has made violent efforts in the past to understand the other.

More than a century ago, an Irish immigrant arrived, barefooted, in Glasgow, during a time of riot. When he stepped on to the quay, he was struck on the head by a loaf. It was a symbolic reception. Glasgow gave him food which he found hard to procure at home, but the food was given without any circumstance of gracious welcome. It was even more significant that the man who threw the loaf neither meant to feed the immigrant nor to assault him. The immigrant just happened to be in the way.

The immigrants had certain qualities which were invaluable for a rapidly expanding city. Their physical strength and hardihood and energy were beyond question. They were ready to bear with primitive conditions of work and living, to toil heavily and to take considerable physical risks if they had the chance of sending a few shillings home to their parents or dependants.

> "Here we are, two Irish labourers
> Just new over from the sod.
> All we want is work and wages.
> We're the boys can carry the hod."

The claim of the old popular song was fully justified. The Irish labourers would tackle anything. They set an example of daring in descending the deep new pits, and they showed a cheerful disregard of the dangers of dynamite. They were the shock troops of the industrial offensive.

But in the view of the Scottish proletariat they asked for too little in the way of wages and were willing to do too much in the way of work. It was natural that the Scots should be resentful and equally natural that the Irish should fail to understand why. The Irish peasant who consumed the most part of what he produced and bartered the rest did not need a great deal of cash, but the small sum he did need he needed most acutely. A pound transferred from Scotland to Ireland multiplied its value several times. The Scottish workers who were used to living in a purely money economy could not well understand the modest demands of Irish workers who were used to an economy in which money played a subordinate but still vital part. The money sent home from Scotland might go into a jug on the dresser, to be doled out sparingly for the few transactions which demanded cash payments, or to be hoarded to pay the fare of one of the family to America. Just as people to-day will make sacrifices to earn "hard" currency, the Irish of a century and a half ago would make sacrifices to earn currency of any kind. Money to them was worth more than its face value.

It was for that reason that they were willing to carry the hod. But the man who carries the hod is the unskilled man. Except for a handful of tailors and shoemakers, the Irish were unskilled workers. (As farm labourers they were more variously skilled than the Scots, but they were labourers, not farmers.) It is a depressing fact that those just removed from poverty are more intolerant of poverty than anybody else. This has been observed during both of the great wars of our generation. It was the working man turned soldier who looked down his nose with the greatest contempt for the ragged and barefooted Arab or Indian, and showed the greatest disapproval of the Belgian or German who worked from dawn to dusk.

The same disapproval was shown for the earliest immigrants. These poor and mostly illiterate men were thought to be only too ready to undertake arduous and dangerous toil in unnecessarily rough conditions. It was a complaint of the Irish that the men and women who came over every year to help with the Scottish harvest were often housed in disgraceful conditions, but the Scottish working man thought that if the conditions were no particular credit to the farmer they were also no credit to the harvesters who meekly put up with them. The Irish were pitifully unorganized, partly because they were not reconciled to permanent settlement in Scotland and partly because they came from a land that had virtually no native institutions. The very virtues of the Irish which won the patronizing approval of the Scottish capitalist earned the not unnatural resentment of the Scottish working man. The working man thought with some justice that the cheap and ready Irish labour was a threat to his own living standards and bargaining power. It was too much to ask him to understand that the threat came from economic circumstances and not from ill-will or class treachery on the part of the immigrants. The threat was there, and was magnified in the proletarian imagination, and that was enough. Careful study of cause and effect is not a proletarian quality.

It was inevitable that the first generation of the immigrants should be unskilled. It was not inevitable that the second and third generations should also be unskilled, but they were. When the Irish immigrants were thrifty and abstinent, they were thrifty and abstinent for the sake of sending money "home". When the native Scots were thrifty and abstinent they were seeking to improve their own condition in Scotland. Many of the poorest Scots "got on" to an astonishing degree. "Getting on" is not the sum of human virtue, but it does demand some steadiness of purpose and strength of character. If the Scots attached too much importance to material progress, the Irish attached too little.

Poverty did not fully explain the failure of the immigrants to apprentice their boys, or the failure of the boys themselves to take advantage of the modest opportunities offered by night schools. The native Scots have always set an honourable example by their readiness to make sacrifices to instruct themselves. Some of the greatest of Scottish scholars have come from homes of genuinely abject poverty. Men of great talent have followed light and learning when they might have followed wealth instead. To-day some of the best of the poor students of Glasgow University bear Irish names.

That is significant. Silently and insensibly the allegedly Irish population have adopted the manners, the habits of mind and the ambitions of the Scots. Assimilation is by no means complete, but it has gone much further than either side recognizes. The great-grandchildren of the exiles from Erin have still something to learn from the Scots, but the Scots have also something to learn from them. A brawling and boozing unskilled labourer in the Gorbals may earn the disapproval of a Kirk elder, and not unjustly. But the Kirk elder might recognize that there are people in the Gorbals of the deepest and simplest religious faith, and that, with the exception of a few orthodox Jews, they are nearly all Catholics.

Temperamentally, the Irish of the early nineteenth century were not well adapted to industrial conditions. Nothing in their previous experience qualified them to make the best of slum conditions or to make the best of a purely money economy. Eighty years ago, a young immigrant walked into a Cowcaddens pub. A bleary-eyed old man welcomed him. "You're just over, son," he said. "When I was your age, I was just like you, blue-eyed and red-cheeked. Look at me now—red-eyed and blue-cheeked."

The old man was one of a fairly heavy casualty list. But the indignant propagandist who flings about statistics of crime and poverty like confetti, though with a less amiable purpose, would do well to reflect that Glasgow, on the whole, has got its money's worth out of the immigrants. There has been too much grumbling on both sides, too much censoriousness on the one and too much excuse-mongering on the other.

Controversy is now idle. The Catholic population in Glasgow is bedded down. It is there, it is large, it is growing, and it cannot be got rid of by any methods short of those favoured by Herr Himmler. It is the essence of intelligent politics to make the best of a situation which cannot be altered. Glasgow has not been altogether successful in handling the immigrant problem. There are large historical reasons why this should be so, but the large historical reasons should now be dropped in the ashcan and a start made on facing facts as they are.

In fact, the problem is well on the way to solving itself if people would only shut up all round. At no time did the immigrant population lack friends who could rise above prejudice and give public-spirited and impartial help to those with whom they had no natural affinity. At no time did the immigrant population lack enemies, the most active being fellow exiles. But to-day, the friends are much more numerous and the enemies are fewer. Nearly every Glasgow Catholic has non-Catholic friends who wish him well, who rejoice at his success and mourn for his failure. The man who feels isolated and out of friendly touch with his neighbours may blame his unfortunate condition on atavistic prejudices, historical survivals and economic circumstances. He may have some justification for his diagnosis. But he would do better for himself and for Glasgow if he made a start by blaming himself.

CHAPTER THIRTEEN

POLITICS

GLASGOW people are highly political. That is to say they hold strong and generally erroneous opinions on all great affairs of State. Their political tradition is fundamentally radical. The workers vote solidly for Socialist candidates who are considered to be the heirs of the old Radicals, although they hold precisely opposite views on most important political matters.

In justice to Glasgow it must be said that the public school Socialists have made no progress at all in capturing Parliamentary seats or leading positions in the Party. Nearly all the Glasgow Socialist Members can clearly, or at least dimly, remember the days when they did some work with their hands. Yet, it must be admitted that these staunch proletarians are mostly a dull lot. They add little to the wit and not much more to the wisdom of the Mother of Parliaments. They make an occasional stodgy speech, infused with a vague secularist humanitarianism, decorated with some painfully obvious quotation from Burns and usually disfigured with some gross or even idiotic misrepresentation of conditions in the Bad Old Days. In the 1950 Parliament, Mr. David Kirkwood found the strength of character to assert that for years on end nobody in Clydebank ate meat. His feelings were hurt when this statement was greeted with unkindly derision. The only Glasgow Socialist Member of distinct personality and independence of mind is Mr. John McGovern of Shettleston.

It was far different in the days immediately following the first World War. Proletarian feeling had been deeply stirred during the War, and it was the efforts of shop stewards and the Labour Withholding Committee which gave Glasgow Socialism its solidly industrial foundation. There were formidable strikes on Clydeside and the Glasgow worker lived in a state of agonized indecision as to whether he hated Lloyd George more than Churchill or Churchill more than Lloyd George. Some of the leaders were clapped for a while in jail and others were deported from the city, but their sufferings were something less than gruesome. A convict of purely civilian status asked Jimmy Maxton what he was in for. Jimmy replied "Sedition". The convict shook his head disapprovingly. "Why didn't you marry the lassie?" he asked.

When the War ended, the Glasgow Socialist bosses were in the highest state of expectation. They had greatly worried the Cabinet, they had forced the hated Churchill to negotiate personally with Davy Kirkwood and even to offer him black bun. They had demonstrated massively in favour of the first Russian Revolution and just as massively in favour of the second. They had made themselves the spearhead of the militant proletariat of Britain, and now the Election gave them their opportunity to cash in politically on their industrial achievements.

John McLean, so much admired by Lenin, was let out of jail to contest Gorbals against a Coalition Labour man, whose name was a hissing and a swearword because he had joined a capitalist Government and supported a capitalist war. McLean enjoyed something of the popularity that Keir Hardie had enjoyed a generation before, but some of the wiser heads (a strictly relative term) thought he was not the best man for the Gorbals. His candidly confessed atheism was no recommendation in a constituency with such a strong Catholic vote and he suffered from another handicap. Although he was an exceedingly nice man in private dealings, he could not mount a platform without going quietly off his head. He was convinced that his jailers had been slowly and deliberately poisoning him. He was equally convinced that the capitalist minions of the Returning Officer would pinch his votes and hide them. He must have read *The Iron Heel* at a period of unusual receptivity.

Jimmy Maxton was considered a certainty for Bridgeton. This former school teacher was an orator of the first class. He had a really good command of humour and a most engaging personality which he knew well how to exploit. He could even gather votes by coughing at suitable moments in an open-air meeting. His appearance was extraordinary. His body was as thin and flat and narrow as the panel of a door. His long lank and greasy hair made him look like an Indian squaw who had lost interest in life and had decided to let everything go. But his voice was deep and musically Scottish, and he could hold any audience with no effort at all. John Wheatley, the housing expert, had none of Jimmy's personal advantages, but he was a first-class debater and it was thought that he could hardly fail to capture Shettleston from a man who was not only shameless enough to be an Admiral but was also in the employment of an armaments firm.

Geographically and politically, Manny Shinwell stood

on the fringe of the Clydeside group. His views were agreeably extreme, but he was thought to be rather too cool and calculating, not at all the man to say anything rash or ill-advised in a burst of generous heat. Nevertheless there were sagacious persons who thought that he might well become Prime Minister when the sainted Ramsay MacDonald went to his well-earned reward.

Hopes ran high, but votes did not. McLean, who had demanded the right to watch over the ballot boxes all night, was washed out in Gorbals. Maxton polled well but was still defeated in Bridgeton, and the loathly Admiral beat Wheatley by a handful of votes. Not even his eminent services in boring the hated Churchill to death could save Davy Kirkwood.

I waited outside the County Buildings in Ingram Street while the results were being declared. Needless to say it was raining. A dejected and elderly man with the look of a lay preacher was hawking an article by Lenin, plaintively asking his British comrades why they were in Murmansk. Out of the fifteen Glasgow seats, only one returned an authentic true-red Socialist. Everywhere else the Beast of the Apocalypse had pulled it off once again. Govan was the "one bright spot" and Neil McLean went off to Westminster alone.

Poor John McLean went back to jail in due course. Not long before his last arrest I heard him speaking in Cathedral Square. Again, needless to say, it was raining. I had a chat with him while he waited for the crowd to gather. He had a beautiful voice and a most modest and sincere courtesy. He knew that sooner or later he would be re-arrested and that he would not come out of jail alive. But he bravely mounted his little platform to bear his burning witness, and highly peculiar witness it was. By this time unemployment had come to Clydeside like the plague, and he asked his audience to join with him there and then in a demonstration. They were to demand that great wooden shelters should be erected in Glasgow Green to give the unemployed cover for their heads, and that very night they were to occupy the crypt of the Cathedral to shelter from the wind and the rain.

It was sad to listen to this silver-haired and silver-voiced man spinning his fantasia. The wall of Duke Street prison was on his left, the dark mass of the Cathedral loomed behind him and on his right the gross bulk of the Royal Infirmary loomed even larger. The rain kept falling with the dreary persistence of a conversational bore. With an equally dreary persistence John McLean developed his theme of the down-trodden proletariat stretching themselves on the pavement for the night to be trodden down even more thoroughly. The audience listened with the genuine respect they always felt for John McLean, but when he called upon them to march over to the Cathedral, there were no takers. They did not fancy sleeping in a draughty crypt when they all had warm beds to go home to, and so home they went.

By that time, John McLean was a lonely figure. He had been appointed Soviet Consul by Lenin, but this honour did not alter the fact that the local Movement had passed him by. The Clydeside Group were now in Parliament. The Election of 1922 brought them rare and refreshing fruit, to counteract the raspberry of 1918. The Socialists captured two-thirds of the Glasgow seats and went off to London primed with combative vigour and self-confidence. They made their last speeches to the light of glaring torches and to the stimulating sound of fervent applause. They looked as if each one of them had his own special Bastille to capture, and they succeeded in making themselves for some years the most talked-of group in Parliament. They had been trained in Glasgow Town Council to make an angry noise on all occasions and to account it for virtue when they succeeded in getting themselves suspended. But their impact on Parliament was much like that of a boxer who hits with the open glove. For a round or two they attracted attention by the noise they made and then they faded out.

They knew about housing. They could speak with authority on that subject, which was of grim interest to Glasgow. But, although they could expose the nature of the great evil, they had nothing of any interest or importance to say when it came to suggesting a method of cure. John Wheatley became Minister of Health in the first Labour Government which was happily short-lived. He had the intelligence to realize that making an angry noise is not the beginning, and much less the end, of statesmanship. His Housing Bill was knocked into shape by numerous Liberal amendments, which he amiably accepted, and he scored one genuine Parliamentary success in a critical debate on the foolishness of George Lansbury. He retired to the back benches long before the second Labour Government took office. His was the only significant contribution made by any of the Clydesiders to the social development of Britain.

The Clydesiders failed because they were not outstandingly intelligent and they had nothing whatever to say. Jimmy Maxton, his hair growing longer, lanker and greasier every year, ended as the most popular Member of the Commons, and the most graceful of all speakers in the vein of friendly compliment on honorific occasions. It was rather a queer ending for the apostle of "Socialism in our time". The fresh-faced and blunt-spoken George Buchanan worked hard at the Pensions Ministry and then retired to a non-political post which he had well earned. Davy Kirkwood became a Privy Councillor, which, for a back-bencher, is the equivalent of being presented with a marble time-piece in recognition of faithful service to the firm. He is now, of course, a peer.

But although the Clydesiders made a diminishing impact on Parliament and gradually lost their influence within the Socialist Party, they consolidated their grip on the constituencies. One Election after another, Maxton returned the smallest expenses of any candidate in Britain. While the campaign was on, he made a few courtesy speeches and then gracefully left it to the tellers to count his majority. It was only the faithful Orange element in Bridgeton that saved his opponents from losing their deposits. The majorities in Gorbals were even more massive, though George Buchanan worked harder for them.

Voting in Glasgow is remarkably steady. Scotstoun, Camlachie, Kelvingrove and Govan are marginal seats where a change of a few hundred votes can win or lose the seat, but Pollok and Hillhead are as safe for the Tories as Gorbals and Bridgeton for the Socialists. Yet, although the Socialists can be sure of a majority of Glasgow seats, the great days were over when the I.L.P. finally foundered and sank. The Glasgow Members are no longer a distinct and distinctive body, and they are of much less interest to the Party bosses than the London Labour Party. Like a cobra, the Commons slowly swallowed and digested the combative Clydesiders and so did Transport House. It is hard luck to be swallowed by two cobras.

But, although the Glasgow Socialists were a heavy disappointment, at least they had authentic local roots and authentic local colour. Their weekly paper, *Forward*, was not the last word in balanced judgment and mature wisdom, but it was as native to the city as any of the commercial papers, and it was lively and often amusing when edited by Tom Johnston, now a truly eminent elder statesman in the grand Radical tradition, but hardly to be counted a thorough Clydesider.

I regret to say that the Conservative (known as the Unionist) Party has no distinctive local quality. It is more sensible and responsible than the Socialist Party, but it rouses no wild emotions except among the Orange section, whose enthusiastic support is an embarrassment in constituencies where the Catholic vote is strong. It is the party of shopkeepers, businessmen and the middle class generally. It is not a Party of Young Tories or Old Tories or any special kind of Tory, and it has yielded up few men of Cabinet rank in recent years.

But it succeeded in recapturing local government for a short time from the Socialists, and that was a considerable achievement. The Moderates (as the Unionists were called before they powdered their faces and called themselves Progressives) held on to a majority in Glasgow Town Council for a considerable number of years after they had lost a majority of Parliamentary seats. The reason was obvious enough. The electors were stimulated by the ructions which the Clydesiders kicked up in Westminster, but they disapproved of the same ructions in George Square. Parliamentary government was

sport, but local government was business, and loud
bawling, desk banging and self-inflicted suspensions
were not thought to be a good way of doing business.
(In the days when Education was controlled by a separ-
ately elected Authority, the Socialists were almost completely washed out at every Election, a clear proof that
the electors took Education more seriously than they
took Socialism.)

The Progressives went down at last to defeat when they
reached an exceedingly ill-advised understanding with the
Scottish Protestant League, and the Socialists occupied
the seats of the mighty in the Council, confident that
they would occupy them till the cows came home. But
it was the chickens that came home and not the cows.
The Socialists were better at local than at national
government but not much. The same men who had been
so boisterous and defiant in opposition roared as gently
as any sucking dove when the Party was in power. The
slums remained and housing promises were unfulfilled.
Tubs were still thumped and voices grew hoarse with
carefully sustained emotion, but Glasgow began to yawn.
The majority dwindled and eventually disappeared.
There was a tremendous hullabaloo when a Progressive
Lord Provost was elected by the votes of two co-opted
members, when the Parties were of equal voting strength,
but at the next Election, the voters gave the Progressives
a small but clear majority.

It cannot be said that the people of Glasgow regard the
City Fathers with undue deference. There is an illumin-
ating comic tale of a carter who asked a pompous-looking
gent to hold his horse for him. "My man," said the
pompous gent, "do you realize I'm a baillie?" "Even

if you are," said the carter, "surely you widnae steal my horse." The anecdote indicates a general suspicion that Glasgow Town Council is not at all times free from corruption. Indeed, at one time suspicion became so voluble that a judicial inquiry was set up by the Government. Evidence of corrupt dealings was invited but none was forthcoming. The Report was therefore negative, but the Judge wisely remarked that it did not follow there was no corruption merely because nobody volunteered to stick his neck out. Indeed, the inquiry had been instituted as a consequence of a Court case which proved the fact of corruption beyond doubt.

All over Britain, municipal government is much more corrupt than national government. It offers more pickings for the man who is tempted to rely on invisible means of support. Surprisingly enough, the principal fomenter of corrupt practices in Glasgow is the Temperance Movement. It is the aim of the professional temperance men to reduce the number of licences by every legitimate means, and they have been highly successful. But every licence which is suppressed, for one reason or another, adds to the value of the licences which remain. A man who holds the licence for a strategically placed pub owns a valuable asset for which he may devoutly thank the enemies of The Trade. But the asset is in continual peril. The licensing rules, particularly the rules governing closing time, are applied with iron rigour. The most honest publican lives in a perpetual state of apprehension, for one slip may cost him a licence worth many thousands of pounds. There is no great need to shed tears for his plight considering that the value of his licence is merely a scarcity value, and a free, if involun-

tary, gift from the very people who prowl round looking
for his destruction.

The extent of corruption is difficult to assess. One or
two scandals which came to Court in fairly recent years
indicated that it goes beyond the matter of public house
licences, but it is more of an irritant than a dangerous
disease. Glasgow has been well served by a large number
of thoroughly honest Councillors who never touched a
dirty penny. At least, there is a refreshing absence of
complacency and humbug about such corruption as
exists. On the rare occasions when a Councillor is
arrested, nobody in Glasgow faints with surprise. Indeed, there is an excessive speculation as to which
other Councillors have managed to beat the rap. When
Topaze, the French comedy on municipal corruption,
was staged in London, a critic said that corruption was
not an English joke because it was not an English fact.
This grown man of at least average mental capacity
sincerely believed what he said. But when *Topaze* was
staged in Glasgow, the audience laughed its head off.
It is doubtful whether simple trust or a high degree of
scepticism is the better attitude for the health of public
administration, but there is no doubt as to what Glasgow's attitude is. It is sceptical.

Indeed, it is unduly so. The interests of the Corporation are so varied and extensive that widespread dis-
honesty would have produced a handsome smash many
years ago. Glasgow Corporation has rivalled Birming-
ham in its municipal enterprise. Its activities range
from printing to farming. The largest single asset is
the transport system, which carries eight hundred
million passengers in the course of a year. At one time,

the Glasgow trams were held up as the finest working model of municipal Socialism in Britain, and everybody in Glasgow believed that theirs was the finest tramway system in the world. The trams were certainly a money-spinner and provided a very cheap and reasonably comfortable service. For years there was stout opposition to the heretical innovators who wanted to bring in buses, but the innovators won in the end, as these restless and unpleasant people so frequently do. They have even succeeded in bringing in trolley buses which scorn the predestinate grooves of the tram lines and make the more solid citizens shake their heads and wonder what the world is coming to. But, in spite of this craze for modernity, this leaping after the latest untried idea (thirty years or so after Darlington) the Glasgow tram still clanks along carrying the main burden of Glasgow transport. Glasgow people have a sentimental affection for their trams, though they are distinctly cool towards the drivers and the conductors. (They are even cooler towards the bus crews.)

Glasgow Transport is the property of a fund called the Common Good. The Common Good is that part of the property of the Burgh which is held by the Corporation for behoof of the community. This means that the revenues from this property may be used more or less as the Town Council thinks fit, but the Town Council's freedom of action is not quite unlimited. Eminent counsel have advised the Corporation (of which the Council is the Executive) that the funds must be applied for the benefit of the community (which would seem to be self-evident), and that the Council must "apply its mind" to each intromission of the funds, and must use "reasonable judgment". Thus, it would be quite illegal for the Council to give the transport system away to some passing stranger in a moment of thoughtless good-nature. As for the making of grants to philanthropic objects, it was sagaciously observed that a decisive factor in deciding reasonable judgment is whether the Common Good can afford it.

In addition to the transport system, the Common Good owns Glasgow Green, a bakers' dozen of public halls, a large estate on Loch Lomond and what are wistfully described as "numerous valuable if at present not too remunerative properties".

Glasgow Green is the oldest public space in Glasgow. In days when what would now be known as graft was the only serious business of the Corporation, an enterprising attempt was made to sell the Green to a private buyer for almost nothing. Even before Burgh Reform, when the Corporation was a quiet family affair, this was rather too much for the citizens and the deal was cancelled. Two centuries ago, the washerwomen who used the Green used to startle visitors by the abandon with which they lifted their skirts while tramping on their sheets and blankets. Women still spread their washing there, but customs and costumes have so changed that they would now have to stand on their heads if they were seeking to attract attention. It was on the Green that James Watt first thought of the separate condenser, and many earnest politicians have thought of more startling ideas before and since. The Green used to be the gathering point of the dismal May Day celebration, and it is the nearest thing Glasgow has to a Speakers' Corner on the model of Hyde Park.

If it is less entertaining than the Hyde Park space, the reason is creditable. The people of Glasgow, it must be insisted again, are considerably more intelligent than the people of other cities. Therefore the speeches, the questions and even the interruptions have at least some intelligible consistency and convey meaning, if not sense. The serious-minded are not afflicted by what they hear, but there is no great entertainment for those whose taste in street corner oratory runs to what Oberon Quin called "a rich badness". But the man who likes to hear the same thing said over and over again with the heavy and remorseless emphasis of a stone-crusher will have ample satisfaction.

The Green is not beautiful. In fact, it is not far from ugly, and the surrounding buildings are on the whole depressing. The neat and unobtrusive Morgue is no doubt a good piece of functional architecture, but its associations are not frivolous, and the proletariat regard the Court House standing in Jail Square at the edge of the Green as representing something worse than death. On the top of that building, the eminent Doctor Pritchard, wearing a frock coat and displaying the greatest aplomb, was publicly hanged. He was an admirable murderer, showing always a brisk and beaming ruthlessness highly suitable in a busy general practitioner. In a mood of surprising sensitiveness, the Council changed the name of Jail Square to Jocelyn Square (Jocelyn being a Papist bishop of long ago). But Jocelyn means nothing to the ordinary citizen, while the word "jail" means a good deal. So, Jail Square it remains and shall remain. Glasgow is a practical town.

By far the most beautiful of Glasgow's parks is Ardgoil. It is four or five times as big as all the other parks put together, but as it lies along one side of an Argyllshire loch, it is not altogether convenient for the children of Bridgeton or the Gorbals.

One of the most notable failures of Glasgow local government has been in the provision of open spaces within the city. A city of crowded tenement buildings has need of much more than the normal amount of park and garden and playing space, but Glasgow has much less. The failure is of the past, and cannot now be remedied, but the people of Glasgow are hardly aware of the deficiency, except the deficiency of playing grounds for youths and children. Glasgow has always been miserly of space and disinclined to leave ground covered with nothing more valuable than grass. It goes almost without saying that open ground is scarcest where it is most needed, which is in the slum areas.

The slums must also be counted a failure for local government. It is true that the slums were put up in days when nobody thought it was the business of a Corporation to house the people, but it was intolerable that ground-greedy builders should ever have been permitted to squeeze one tenement building in between two others. Even in a city where space has never been sufficiently valued and the cost of house rent has always been grudged, this economy was a mortal offence against health and civilized living. Some of the worst of these back lands were in George Street, hardly more than a stone's throw from the City Chambers, and the human derelicts of these appalling buildings spilled on to the benches of George Square, where their evident moral and physical ruin offered a picturesque medieval contrast to the prosperous baillies coming out to do the City's business.

Tearing down these horrible and stifling blocks, though it was long delayed, was the least of the problem. The greater difficulty was to find alternative building sites elsewhere. The difficulty was not chiefly created by the grasping landowners of Socialist propaganda but by the nature of the surrounding terrain, which is mostly hilly, and by the spending habits of the people. For working-class families who had been conditioned to the heat of the slums and had never spent more than a tiny fraction of their income in travelling to work in the close-packed city, a house on a windy ridge, at a considerable distance from work, had weighty disadvantages. An airy brick house standing on a windy space was very much colder than a stone slum in a tight huddle of other slums. Not only was more heating required, but there were more rooms to be heated. In the years when money was cruelly hard to come by, a new house came near to wrecking the family budget, and indeed there was a small drift back to the slums. Many of the new houses were insufficiently heated because the people could not afford much coal. The householder transferred from a slum had to pay a higher rent and had to meet much heavier travelling expenses. The extra demands on his earnings did not leave much for fuel, and now when paper money is more plentiful, the fuel cannot be procured.

Much could have been done to ease the grim housing situation if existing tenement houses had been recon-verted. Two small slum houses knocked together and modernized would have made one decent house. But the simple common-sense of this housing method made no headway against the strong popular dislike of house-owners and house-factors. It was not practical politics to proceed with any scheme that might be construed as helping the landlord or the factor.

The house-factor is considerably ahead of the police in the unpopularity competition. He is conceived as an economic Sir Jasper, twisting a sinister bowler instead of an evil moustache and seeking by every means to squeeze the last usurious farthing from the wretched proletariat. They have stones where other humans have hearts, and the widow's tear merely makes them yawn when it does not make them snarl.

It is undoubtedly true that Glasgow house-factors are not strikingly sentimental, but it is also true that they would not last long in the job if they were. A considerable number of their customers show a marked disinclination to pay their rents, and some of them take a singularly light-hearted view of their responsibilities to avoid unnecessary damage to the house they occupy. If a house-factor discovers that parts of the kitchen coal bunker have been chopped up for firewood he may be excused for expressing himself with some testiness. House factors are but mortal men, from which it follows that some are good, some bad and some indifferent. This conclusion is obvious enough, but is not well received in Cowcaddens and Gorbals.

In the matter of Glasgow housing, the most thorough exploiters of the poor have been the poor themselves. After the first World War there was a small wave of rent strikes. A woman who was threatened with eviction and who called on high heaven or the Socialist Party to save her, was found to be charging for one room in her house more than the rent she refused to pay for the whole dwelling. To-day in the South Side of Glasgow there are tenements of fairly large houses which are still in good enough order but have sagged perceptibly in the social world. A number of these houses have been taken over by Indians who have let them room by room. There is, of course, only one lavatory and only one kitchen. It is housing on the Moscow level, and exploitation on the Asiatic level, by gentlemen who have a sad-eyed and generally resigned appearance of submitting themselves to the cruel yoke of the dominant white races. The key of some of these rooms can be hired from day to day, or from hour to hour, for purposes which may be easily conjectured. This is perhaps natural enough. When a people have been house-trained for centuries in submission to tyranny and exploitation, and have enjoyed only a historically brief period of just (i.e., British) rule, it is not surprising that they should seek to exploit and tyrannize on their own account when they get a chance. But they really ought to look more cheerful about it. The Downtrodden Look is appropriate to those who are being downtrodden, but is offensive in those who are downtreading.

The housing problem of Glasgow is not a product of war destruction, or of the shifts and growth of population since the War. It is a venerable and an appalling problem. Before the War only one town in England came within half the over-crowding ratio that was a commonplace in Glasgow and neighbourhood. War damage in Glasgow was slight, but the halt in building has left the city worse off for quantity, though not for quality, of accommodation than it was before the War began. Some of the vilest Cruikshanks slums have been wiped out, but rising prices and laggard building have made a grim problem even grimmer. A woman in a really detestable slum secured a place on the housing list when her girl was a toddler. She is now off the housing list, not because she has got a house, but because her girl is now twenty-one. However, she has serious hopes that the appalling tenement in which she lives will soon be condemned as unfit for human habitation, and she will be moved before the roof falls down on her.

Even when all propaganda cant has been discounted, the housing problem is still deplorable, and it must dominate local politics for many years to come. Other issues may assume a temporary importance, but the great permanent and intractable evil is housing. The slums are partly the producers and partly the product of disease, ignorance and irresponsibility. The responsibility of clearing the slums has been landed fairly in the lap of the Town Council. It will lie in that lap for a very long time.

While the Council has had to accept this unwelcome burden, its powers have been closely shorn in other ways. The Health Act has taken away most of the Council's medical work, and the nationalization of gas and electricity has taken away from Council control two departments, very much to the disadvantage of the citizen. With plentiful supplies of coal at whistling distance and with an extremely compact area to serve, Glasgow Electricity was able to give a service which was highly efficient and almost startlingly cheap. For one reason or another, gas was not so well handled, but national ownership has been a misfortune for Glasgow people, whether they use gas or electricity, or both.

Even when these departments have been taken away, the Town Council is still the biggest employer in Glasgow. Nearly forty thousand men and women are main-

tained in full-time permanent employment, and many
thousands more on a temporary basis. When to these are
added Government employees of all kinds and the workers
for public bodies like the Clyde Trust it may be suggested
that the late Jimmy Maxton saw more Socialism in his
time than perhaps he suspected.

The Town Council has shown much enterprise, sometimes well and sometimes ill-advised, and has taken on
a large variety of responsibilities. The rosy dream that a
Socialist-dominated Council would speedily create a
New Jerusalem in the Gorbals was dissipated shortly
after the Council became Socialist-dominated. But the
Socialist Party have now got back to power, for a reason
which is also the reason why Glasgow working-class
housing is still a scandal. The Progressives proposed
to offer a number of Council-built houses for sale. This
was a move of ordinary justice and ordinary common
sense, for in Glasgow as elsewhere the taxpayers and rate-
payers are paying part of the house rent for people of
comfortable and more than comfortable means. (It was
revealed that one Glasgow Council tenant had an income
of three thousand a year, plus five hundred expenses.)
In vain did Progressive candidates argue that every house
sold was a relief to the rates, and in vain did they point
out that a remarkable number of Socialist Councillors
were enjoying a rent subsidy. There were demonstrations
and threats of strikes, and the Socialists were returned
on the claim that it was the blackest reaction to interfere
with the sacred principle of something for nothing. It
was a curious and saddening instance of how far bitterness
and bigotry have penetrated the proletarian mind.

CHAPTER FOURTEEN

THEY BELONG TO GLASGOW

POLITICAL, racial and social divisions are easy to be observed in Glasgow, and they occasionally create a degree of ill-temper which is little short of naughty, but there is a unity of outlook and character which is not so easily observed, but is undeniably there.

However, the surface variety is more obvious. Across the stairhead in a dingy working-class tenement, there may be two families, one with a son lecturing in a University, and the other with a son in jail. In a suburb of small villas, there may be two houses side by side, one named "Rowena" because the woman has romantic and unsatisfied yearnings, and the other named "Rangoon" because the man spent most of his working life in Burma.

The cheerful toiler swaying slightly along Argyle Street on a Saturday night is likely to be a fervent lover of the Rangers, but there is a good chance that he is a fervent hater. He may regard the Pope with the warmest trust, affection and reverence, or he may view him in quite a different light. The earnest man in elder's blacks may be indeed an elder, but he may also be a serious-minded propagandist for atheism.

So far as physical appearance goes, the class distinction is clear enough. The middle-class business man is a big fellow with a taste for heavy suits, brown shoes and an umbrella. He may lunch at Lang's or Danny Brown's, or at his funereal club, if he is one of the bigger men. His political ideas are soundly Conservative, mainly because he sees no future in supporting ideas which are soundly Liberal. He thinks that he ought to have more money than he has, and he darkly suspects that some of the working class would be well enough paid if they got a good deal less money than they do.

But he is no stranger to the working class. He knows them and understands them. It is not possible for him to live the life of Brahmin-like seclusion from the manual workers which is led by quite a number of London business and professional men. It would never occur to him to claim any intrinsic superiority over the proletariat, nor would it occur to the proletariat to concede him any. As he walks along the street some little casual labourer with an eighth of an unlit Woodbine in his mouth will call out "See's a light Mac" in a friendly and unembarrassed manner. The fine shades and divisions of the English caste system mean no more to the middle classman than they do the riveter in John Brown's or the Govan boiler-scaler.

His wife may be rather more conscious of class distinctions and may secretly wish that life in Glasgow was rather more like life in the Tatler. But she hopes for a vain thing. In Glasgow, *Tatler* life is as unreal as Hollywood life and a good deal less interesting. She may try to create a "set", with exclusive little groups for bridge and canasta and cocktails at exclusive times in exclusive American bars, but nobody will even know that the set exists, and there is no bar so exclusive that it is not likely to be invaded by men who will plunge into a discussion on water-tube boilers or marine insurance and will show a coarse indifference to the little pretensions of a little imitation Mayfair.

No wealthy Glasgow man need feel socially handicapped because he is "in trade". On the contrary, if a wealthy man is not in trade, there are likely to be uncomfortable speculations as to where he got his money. In places like Kilmacolm, Bridge of Allen and Bridge of Weir, the men of commercial property may endeavour with some success to merge into the class of men of landed property, but the more successful they are, the further are they removed from Glasgow.

The absence of class feeling in Glasgow is partly caused by the fact that the city is intensely, uncompromisingly and predominantly industrial. On its Eastern side it is ringed with pits, and closely tied with the Black Country of Lanarkshire. The great derricks of the shipyards are the most conspicuous structures in the city, and at night the air is luridly lit by the blast furnace of Blochairn. It is impossible to escape from industrialism anywhere in Glasgow. Industrialism conditions the mentality of Glasgow men, even those who use no heavier machinery than fountain pens and typewriters.

Any port town must have a certain cosmopolitan flavour, but the Glasgow flavour is specially strong, for Glasgow sent her sons abroad in a great variety of occupations. Glasgow produces wireless operators, marine engineers, chartered accountants, civil engineers, doctors, teachers, oil men, estate managers and planters, and they are ready to go far afield in search of a good job. Some of them are naturally lost to Glasgow for ever, but a large number come back from coral strands or frozen wastes, to resume the cloth cap or the bowler hat and take up with renewed assurance their old place in their community group, or perhaps go one step higher. A vast number of the London proletariat are blankly unaware of anything beyond their own borough, but there are Glasgow men who may never have crossed the Clyde to Rutherglen but can learnedly discuss the pubs of Hongkong and Shanghai or the proper way of treating native servants in Calcutta.

STREET BOOKIE "THE WIDOW'S MITE"

The artisan calls no man his superior, but he sometimes finds it difficult to disguise his belief that the unskilled man is his inferior. Life in the slums may have a rich wildness of its own, but the artisan suspects that it is lacking in a due degree of prudence, providence and balance. He may accept it as a political axiom that all that is wrong with the slums is caused by the System, but he has a secret suspicion that some of what is wrong with the slums is caused by the people who live there. This suspicion is deeply felt if uncontrollable circumstances compel him to live in or near the slums.

Nevertheless, in the pub, the tram or on the football terracing, the unskilled man is a brother, and no one would have it otherwise. That is why, although social communication in Glasgow is not always genial, it is always unembarrassed. All sorts and conditions in Glasgow have more in common than they consciously understand.

In an important sense, they all do belong to Glasgow. There is the girl coming out into the rain from Dennistoun Palais, her eyes still dancing, and the girl from a more expensive dance hall, tapping a silver slipper, snuggling into her fur coat and waiting for the car to be driven round. They go different ways home, but the most important difference between them is money. It is not a big difference.

The man who shivers with a rug round his knees, shouting for "Academicals" or "High", and the man bawling his head off behind the Rangers goal have much the same view of the meaning of sport. The men gravely discussing share dividends in the Grosvenor Bar are of the same kind as the men gravely discussing Pool Dividends in "Wines, McManus, Spirits". So it is with the crowds at the dog tracks and the earnest spectators crouching through the tobacco smoke to follow the amateur boxing in the L.M.S. Rovers' Hall. So it is with the students of all degrees, poring over book barrows or swotting in the melancholy light of "the Mitchell".

The mighty and terrifying roar at Hampden on International Day, Saint Andrew's Cathedral packed to the door with men and women going to Confession on Christmas Eve, the lights blazing all night on Hogmanay, Peter Colin Neil Blair MacIntyre setting the world to rights at Govan Cross, the Highlanders gathered under the Central Station Bridge, couples meeting at the Central Station Shell, journalists exchanging wise thoughts in Ferrari's, brutal capitalists stretched out in the armchairs of the Western Club, the earnest intelligentsia trudging up to the University for a night-time lecture, they are in many respects far apart, but they are also in many respects remarkably united, in speech, in social outlook and social custom.

They have a large inheritance. It was in Glasgow that the decisions were taken which precipitated the Civil War and the death of King Charles the First (a Dunfermline man). It was in Glasgow that Oliver Cromwell was discouraged, if not positively cowed, in argument. It was here also that the genial Adam Smith returned to his social club flushed and discomposed because he had just called Doctor Johnson a son of a bitch, admittedly under high provocation. About the same time, James Watt secured the patent for his "fire-engine" which was to prove of some importance to the world.

From the fire engine came the steamship, and the steamship made the Clyde the father of all waters. Some solid work in the slave trade, in cotton, in prairie farming, in coal, iron and highly competent running of other people's affairs yielded large dividends. All the seas and oceans and the continents owe something to Glasgow, and Glasgow has quietly seen that the dues were paid. It is an international city, familiar with what Brisbane requires and with what Bilbao is ready to sell. It is also a provincial city, more than half convinced that niggers begin at Kilmarnock. It is a city which prefers New York to London and vaguely understands that Manchester is at one end of a well-known canal.

It is a city where it rains a lot, where the air is always sharp, and where Sunday is a dismal theological hangover. In Eglinton Street, the bells toll to the unheeding groups at the tram stops, casting their great reverberant, expanding cones of sound, reminding men of the Chief End of Man, but reminding them in vain. A ship's siren sounds from the river, more melancholy still, but more significant, for James Watt's fire engine and what followed it have lasted better than the Shorter Catechism. But yet more significant is the clang of the bell as a tram draws up, clanking and grinding, at the top. The church bell may stir something half forgotten in the heart. The ship's siren stirs something very alive in the mind. But it is the tram bell that has the ring of the homely, familiar and reassuring thing. The huddle at the stop move forward and step on to the car, bound for their villas in Pollokshields or their tenement houses in the neighbourhood of Eglinton Toll. They have no appearance of vivacity and they do not chatter aimlessly, but they have a quiet and solid assurance, a sense of well-being and a confidence in their own future and the future of their city. Why would they not?

They belong to Glasgow and Glasgow belongs to them.